Hannah's Story

Book 1:
The Love After Loss Series

Danette Fogarty

Losing a parent is a like losing a piece of oneself. The person you identify yourself with; personality traits like your sense of humor, or physical traits like eye color, hair color, the shape of your toes, or anything else that reminds you, or someone else, of that person.
Thank you, Dad, for teaching me some very difficult lessons, for showing me how to laugh at just about anything, and for teaching the boys and I what we want to leave behind.

Thank you, Megan!

Three women, all suffering from losing
a loved one
get an invitation to a retreat in Galveston, Texas.
Hannah has just lost her father, after a long battle
with ALS.
Not knowing what to do with herself after
being a caretaker for so long, Hannah accepts the
invitation. She is lost as far as what she wants to
do with the rest of her life and happens
upon a father and his daughter on the beach.
Asher Kelley was trying to teach his six year-old
daughter, Skyler, about sea life in the
Gulf of Mexico when he is helped by this
beautiful woman passing by and helping him
save a turtle. Asher is no stranger to loss
and offers to listen if Hannah needs to talk.
Can two people, who meet by happenstance, find the
Love After Loss they seek?

Chapter 1

"It's okay, Dad," Hannah whispered to her father. His breathing was noticeably shallower today. His hospice nurse, Chris, told Hannah that they were at the point where he would need to decide for himself if, and when, he wanted to go on. And by "go on," Hannah knew that meant to die.

Tears streaked down her face as she looked at her father, a mere shell of the man she'd known growing up. Oh, he'd been one of those "larger than life" men, the kind that played sports, took out the trash with only one hand, killed any bug that scared her, and even checked under the bed for monsters. He was also the only parent she had left, so losing him was something Hannah hadn't been able to come to terms with just yet.

She walked out of her father's room and into the living room. It still remained as it had after her mother's death, a decade before. The same rose patterned material covered the sofa, the wall color was the same, and even the same coffee table books remained. It was as if time stood frozen for the last ten years.

And now, her father would be with her mother soon, and she.......well, she would be alone.

Tears fell down her cheeks as she looked out the large bay window. It was late May and the weather was starting to get warm and muggy. In southeast Texas, the winter months weren't really cold, and it seemed to shift from cool evenings, to hot muggy ones in the space of a few weeks or so.

She sat there for a while, trying to take all of this in, but it was so difficult.

Eight years ago, her father called her at college, and told her he needed her to come home.

Thinking about the conversation made Hannah sigh, mainly because she'd been truly unkind and selfish during that call. He didn't give her a reason why he wanted her to come home, so she'd given him at least a half dozen why she couldn't. What it came down to was, she didn't want to go home.

College was her salvation. She'd spent the last two years of high school keeping house and making sure her father was taken care of after her mother passed away. Going away, even if it was only four hours away to college, in Corpus Christi was a blessing. At college she felt normal, only feeling the pressures of exams and papers she had to get done for her classes. When her father called, demanding she come home, she hadn't been ready to give that up.

She promised him she'd come home after the semester was over, and he agreed.

Only a year and a half after leaving, Hannah found herself home once again. But this time was different, her father did need her.

"I have ALS," He told her, very solemnly.

Not having any idea what that was, Hannah only stared at him blankly. "What's ALS?" She'd asked him.

Frank Whitman sat down at the kitchen table and explained his condition to his daughter. "Basically, my brain will stop sending the messages to my muscles that tells them to work." He began, "And I will eventually die from this."

Even having him say the words, Hannah wouldn't accept them. "No!" She shouted and got up from the table and ran up to her room.

Hours later, she came downstairs to find her father still sitting at the kitchen table, cradling his head in his hands. He looked up when he heard Hannah come in, tears in his eyes. "I'm sorry," He muttered, before standing up and hugging his daughter.

Snapping back to the present, as she heard Chris enter the living room, Hannah looked up at the hospice nurse and smiled. Chris had been a Godsend the last couple of weeks, giving Hannah a much-needed break.

Her father now required round-the-clock care. They no longer went out to doctor's appointments since the disease was affecting almost all of his motor functions. The doctors explained that, eventually, it would affect his breathing and her father would die. Still not wanting to think about that yet, Hannah stood, and asked Chris, "Would you like some lunch?"

Nodding, Chris followed Hannah into the kitchen. It was all white, and galley style. He sat at the breakfast bar, and watched Hannah fix them some sandwiches. "How are you holding up?" He asked her as she handed him a plate and nodding his thanks.

Taking a deep breath, Hannah replied, "I'm okay." She meant it, because she was okay, she wasn't the one withering away in a bed from a disease.

"There are some great grief counseling groups around here," Chris said quietly, and slid a business card across the bar.

Hannah nodded, but didn't pick up the card, or even reply. She wasn't ready…..not yet, to discuss the "after" part of her father's life. When she was, well, then she'd do what she had to for herself.

Chris understood Hannah's need for quiet. All too often, he watched as family members were as stressed physically and emotionally as the ill patients he helped them take care of. The patients were able to find peace eventually, but the family members were left with grieving, and that was the hard part. "He talks about your mother a lot now," He said to Hannah, trying to make small talk.

Looking over the bar, Hannah smiled, and answered, "Good." She couldn't say anything else, for fear she'd break out into sobs. After eating half of her sandwich, which was a good effort on her part these days, she pushed away from the bar and cleaned up the small mess left from lunch preparations. When she turned around again, Chris was gone; probably in with her father.

The house was quiet. Too quiet, and she missed the sounds of her mother cooking in the kitchen and her father yelling at sports teams on the television. Her childhood was so light and happy, and she had no idea it would turn into this………tomb.

She went down the hallway and into her father's room. It was the den at one time, but they put in the hospital bed, and an ever-increasing collection of medical equipment when he was no longer able to get upstairs to his bedroom.

Slipping into the room, Hannah stayed against the wall as Chris helped her father through his breathing treatments. It wasn't difficult to see that Frank was losing his strength faster than predicted. Tears slipped down Hannah's cheeks as she watched her father try to hang on. She knew in her heart that he was hanging on for her.

Later that evening, during her turn to stay with her dad, while Chris went home and before the next hospice nurse came in, Hannah sat at her father's bedside while he rested.

She was reading for a while, but the story just couldn't hold her attention. She turned on the television and flipped through the channels trying to find something interesting to watch. She had just turned onto a channel that had The Golden Girls on when she heard her father make a noise. Looking over, she saw that he was smiling at something one of the characters said. Sitting back in her chair, she left the show on, listening to the witty comments of the cast, and smiling herself when she heard her father's soft laugh.

"Hannah," The night hospice nurse whispered, "I'm here so you can go to bed."

Roused from her sleep, Hannah took a moment to get her bearings. "Hi, Rosie," She smiled, and stood up to stretch.

Her father was sleeping peacefully, with a hint of a smile on his face. "He had a good evening," She told Rosie, before leaning over to kiss her father on the forehead.

Rosie smiled, and waved her hands at Hannah, saying, "Shoo now and get some rest."

Not wanting to mess with Rosie, or anyone at this point, Hannah nodded in agreement and went upstairs.

She walked into her room, and turned on the small lamp on the nightstand. Even after her father couldn't come upstairs, and insisted that Hannah take the master bedroom with the adjoining bathroom, she refused.

It was as if accepting that change in their situation meant his death was imminent. Her room, much like the rest of the house, was unchanged since her return from college. Her A&M banner was still pinned up on the wall and her trophies from softball in high school still stood on the shelf her father hung for her. This room, was as stuck as Hannah was, in the flux of merely existing.

A week later, Hannah's aunt Ruth, her father's sister, arrived. Since her dad was now declining daily, it was time to call in what little family they had left. Her grandparents passed away when Hannah was small, from a car accident, so his only relative was his sister, Ruth. She was a slip of a woman, not more than five feet tall, but she had a voice that could penetrate cement block.

"Hannah," Ruth boomed out as she came in the front door, and took her niece into a tight embrace.

Smiling, Hannah said, "Auntie Ruth," back and wanted to cry at the sight of a friendly face.

Stepping back, Ruth took a look at her niece, and shook her head. The girl looked at least ten years older than her age of twenty-seven, and clearly wasn't taking care of herself. If she lost any more weight, she'd be darn near invisible. "Girl," Ruth clucked her tongue, "you aren't taking time for yourself."

Not wanting to cry a measly few minutes after her aunt's arrival, Hannah tried to smile in an effort to brush it off. "I'm fine," She answered.

Ruth didn't believe Hannah for one second. She sighed, and asked, "Where's my big brother?"

They walked down the hall toward the den, and Hannah tried to prepare her aunt, by saying, "He's very frail, and doesn't move much now."

It was apparent, at least to Hannah, that her aunt either didn't believe her, or just wasn't ready to see Frank in his present condition. "Oh, Lord," She said under her breath when she saw her brother. Shoring up her shoulders, Ruth bellowed, "There's the most handsome brother in the world!" and went over to Frank's bedside.

Both Chris and Hannah wanted to give her father and Ruth some time to visit so they quietly left the room.

When Hannah was outside of the room, she fell against the wall of the hallway, almost knocking down a picture of her family that hung up there. Chris was at her side immediately, and helped her the rest of the way into the living room, and sat her down on the sofa. "I'll get you some water," He said, and went into the kitchen.

Still in a daze, Hannah could only smile weakly as he put the glass in her hands, and guided it up to her lips. The cool liquid felt good against her dry throat. She waited a few moments, then nodded to Chris, letting him know she was okay. He sat down across from her, ready to help if she needed it. Finally, Hannah looked over at him, and said, "I'm not ready."

Chris's heart broke for her, he could see it, witnessed the denial all the time in his job. "I know," He answered, then added, "He knows it too."

That last bit of information surprised Hannah. She asked Chris, "How do you know that?"

"It's not just your mother he talks about, it's you too," Chris started, "he's worried that you won't know what to do after he's gone."

Curious, Hannah asked him, "What do you tell him?"

Chris thought for a moment, then answered, "It varies, some days I tell him that you'll go back to college," he smiled, "and some days I am honest and tell him that you'll have a hard time of it, but eventually you'll figure out your way." He reached over and patted Hannah's hand, "Because I believe you will find your way."

Feeling sarcastic, and full of self-pity, Hannah replied, "I'm glad one of us thinks so."

They could hear snippets of conversation coming from her father's room. Mostly it was Ruth's voice, carrying like a loud speaker, but it was upbeat, and full of love, so they were sure that Frank appreciated his sister being here.

A half hour later, Ruth came out of the room, and plopped down on the sofa next to Hannah. "He's weak, but he's still fighting," She said nonchalantly. Looking at her niece, Ruth asked, "Can you show me to my room please?"

Hannah nodded and walked with her aunt upstairs. All the furniture from the den was jammed into the spare bedroom so Hannah put her aunt in her parents' bedroom. She didn't miss the look of surprise her aunt shot her, but let it go. They were all having to deal with the unpleasantness of the situation. "I've changed the sheets, and aired it out," Hannah told her aunt as they walked into the room.

"It is just fine," Ruth replied. She set down her bag on the bed, and started to unpack, "He asked about your Uncle Ron and your cousin, Ricky." She smiled as she pulled out a blouse. "He's always worried about other people," Ruth started to choke up as she said it.

Hannah walked over to where her aunt was standing and wrapped her arms around her shoulders, saying, "I know he loves you."

Covering Hannah's hands with her own, Ruth only nodded. She knew her brother loved her and he knew she loved him right back. She was thankful for it. "I'll call Uncle Ron later and give him an update," Looking at Hannah, Ruth smiled, and added, "He can't take off of work until things are done."

Not missing her aunt's meaning, Hannah only shook her head. It seemed that everyone, except her, had a life to live outside of this house and her father. She squeezed her aunt's hand, "I understand, and I'm sure Dad wouldn't want everyone hovering around him anyway." She wanted to make this as easy for everyone else as she could.

Ruth knew that Hannah was the best of both Frank, and his wife, Janine. She had a genuinely good heart, and it broke Ruth's heart to know that Hannah would not have either of her parents when she got married, and had children. While she visited with her brother earlier, she promised him that she would be there for Hannah whenever there was something important that happened in her life.

Smiling, as she remembered her big brother always taking care of her, Ruth knew she could do this for him.

Hannah could see her aunt was remembering something. Perhaps something sweet from her childhood, or a funny anecdote her father always tried to give out, but it was a good thing. She, herself, became lost in the memories from time to time; as if her mother hadn't passed away and her father wasn't terminally ill.

"Why don't you lay down, you look exhausted," Ruth ordered her niece. "I'll take care of your dad until the night nurse gets here."

Confused, Hannah started to say, "Uh, I….." but was silenced by the determined look in her aunt's eyes.

Ruth walked Hannah across the hall, to the door of her bedroom, and all but pushed her niece inside. Sometimes, force was necessary, especially if it was for someone's own good.

Leaning against the door, Hannah shouted, "Just call me if you need anything," and turned around to stare at her room.

Chapter 2

Waking up slowly, it took Hannah a few seconds to get her bearings. She usually woke up early, having slept poorly, and dragged herself through the house to get her father's things ready for the day. When she looked over at the bedside clock, and saw it was after nine in the morning, she flew up and out of bed.

She ran downstairs, barely getting her robe wrapped around her before hurrying into her father's room. As soon as she passed through the doorway, she stopped in her tracks. Her aunt was sitting there, helping Chris feed her father. He was already cleaned up for the day and looked rested himself. "I, uh, I'm sorry I'm up so late," She said to the threesome.

Ruth turned around and smiled at her niece, "It's not your fault; I turned off your alarm." Seeing her niece's temper start to stir, Ruth rushed to answer, "I talked to Chris and Rosie and we all thought you could use the rest and I was more than capable of lending a hand."

Frank, seeing his daughter, smiled. He was only able to make sounds now, not form words, and it frustrated him to no end. "Ha…," he said, using the sound for his daughter's name.

A smile breaking her frown, Hannah walked over, and sat on the side of the bed. "Are you having a good time visiting with Aunt Ruth?"

Giving a small wave, which meant that he wasn't having any, fooling around, Frank smiled at his sister, and then at his daughter.

Hannah knew there wasn't much else she could do right now, so she kissed her father's forehead, then went upstairs to shower and get ready for the day.

An hour later, Hannah came downstairs. She really did feel better. The sleep had done wonders and she didn't see the, usually visual, dark circles under her eyes. With her lighter mood, she chose a pair of shorts and blouse instead of her customary workout clothes.

Chris was doing some paperwork at the kitchen breakfast bar when she entered the room, and looked surprised when he saw her, "Well, you look great," he told her.

"Thank you," Hannah replied. "Do I look bad most days?" She asked him quickly. "Be honest," She told him.

Sighing, Chris answered, "Not bad, it's just that comfort and convenience are easier."

Hannah gave him a look of disbelief, and commented, "So basically you're saying that I haven't been trying because it's too exhausting to make the effort."

Shrugging his shoulders, Chris smiled, and said, "You said it, not me."

She patted him on the shoulder, and walked into the kitchen to make herself some brunch.

Ruth came in a few minutes later, and smiled when she saw her niece. "Hannah, you look rested," She quipped before sitting down at the bar, next to Chris, and wearing a big grin.

Hannah walked over to her aunt and gave her a tight squeeze, "Yes," she replied, "thank you."

Throwing up her hands, Ruth said, "You know, some of us just have the touch."

Smiling at her aunt's sassy remarks felt good. Hannah almost forgot why they were all three here. Almost was the key word, all too quickly, the weight of her father's illness threw itself over her mood, and stole the smile from her face.

Ruth could see the light seep out of her niece's eyes, and her heart broke a little more. This morning Frank was able to tell her that he was almost ready. He didn't say the exact words, but it was the way he looked at her, the sounds were still something she was trying to figure out, but Chris helped her understand most of them. She was relieved that she was able to be here for her brother, and her niece, even though the pain was going to be unbearable.

Her hunger, all but dissipated, Hannah took another bite of her cottage cheese, and then cleaned her dish and spoon before heading into her father's room.

He was sleeping when she entered, the television low in the background. The noise from it barely masked the noise from her father's labored breathing. There were other sounds too, the constant blip sounds from the machine that delivered his intravenous medication and the hum of the oxygen machine that was beside his bed.

Hannah stared at him for a long while. She prayed that he would stay with her longer, and yet felt guilty for being so greedy and wanting him to stay.

Finally, she walked over and sat down beside his bed. There was a book on the table next to it. Picking it up, Hannah noticed it was a biography. She smiled as she read the title. It was about a seal team member and his life. Her father, when he wasn't busy watching sports, had a love of reading. He read books about wars, military history, and the brave men and women who fought for their country. She never understood it, because she preferred more light-hearted subjects, but she remembered fondly, watching him sit on the back porch, and read his books.

She was so lost in her thoughts, that Hannah didn't notice her father was awake. He made a slight noise, and brought her out of her musings. "Hey, dad," She said, and smiled.

Frank watched his daughter, and smiled back. Today, she reminded him so much of his wife, Janine, that he'd almost called her by his wife's name, until the memory of her passing hit him. "Hi," He said in a soft voice to his daughter.

"Can I get you anything?" Hannah asked her father.

Shaking his head yes, Frank made the shape of the letter c with his hand, that meant cup or drink. When his speech started to suffer from the disease, they came up with letters that meant words so he could still communicate.

Hannah reached over and grabbed a cup of water off the table, placed a straw in it, and brought it up to her father's lips. For some reason, he was able to make the necessary movements to drink through a straw and Hannah was thankful for that little victory. It made giving him fluids a lot easier.

Ruth came into the room, smiling widely at her brother. "Well, it's about time you woke up," She teased him.

Rolling his eyes, Frank made the sounds "Fun...ny."

Hannah looked at her father, her face ripe with shock. That was the first full word her father had spoken in almost two months. Maybe her aunt was just the thing he needed to help him hang on a little bit longer.

Sitting down on the opposite side of the bed, Ruth squeezed her brother's hand and smiled, "Okay, what do you want for lunch?" She asked Frank.

Chris had just come in, and was making preparations to help her father by changing his bedding and washing him up. Since Frank was no longer able to get up on his own, he had to wear adult underpants that made him feel like an infant being diapered, or at least that's what he told Chris. Looking first to Hannah, then to Frank, Chris announced, "Okay, guy time, all the ladies out."

Even Ruth didn't argue or tease. She wanted to help her brother keep as much of his personal dignity as he could. As soon as she and Hannah were in the kitchen she asked her niece, "So do you have to help him with his personal stuff too?"

It was a question that, for some reason, people asked. Hannah had been her father's sole caregiver for years so she'd had to help him bathe and even change his underwear. It was not a pleasant task for either of them, but they'd made a pact long ago that Hannah would only help him when absolutely necessary, in order to help them both feel less awkward. "Yes," She answered her aunt's question, "and I think it's more difficult for him than it is for me."

Nodding, Ruth replied, "I'm sorry I asked, I know it's a rude question."

Smiling at her aunt, Hannah told her, "It's asked a lot, and there are a lot of disapproving looks, but we've made this work so far."

A tear slid down Ruth's cheek and she pulled Hannah closer for a hug, "We know you have, and we're so proud of you for taking this on."

Hannah didn't want to cry, not like this, so she held herself straight. "Thank you," She answered, and cleared her throat to hold back the emotion.

Sensing that her niece didn't want this kind of talk, Ruth sighed, and moved away to get some tea from the refrigerator. She poured three glasses, thinking that Chris may want some when he was finished helping Frank. "I'm here until the end," Ruth announced, sitting down next to her niece.

Surprised by her aunt's words, Hannah could only stare at her. "You don't have to stay, you know."

"I want to, Hannah." Ruth explained. "I've talked to my brother about it and he thinks it's a good idea and Lord knows Uncle Ron is having a field day ordering in pizza and watching ESPN nonstop while I'm away."

Chuckling at the vision of her uncle doing just that, Hannah shook her head. "It could be a while," She told her aunt, not wanting to sugar-coat it.

Ruth sat there, looked at her niece, and knew that it wouldn't be long at all. She'd called and spoke to Frank's doctors, his hospice nurses, and him personally. Even though he had a slight reprieve today because of her visit, his time was short. The only person who didn't seem to realize just how short, was Hannah. Refusing to say anything else that might upset her niece, Ruth replied, "That's okay, I'll stay as long as it takes."

The next two days were the same, and Hannah felt so much better. She'd gotten some good sleep and didn't feel worried about her dad as much when Aunt Ruth was there to check on him.

On the third day, however, things started to change. She'd woken up early that morning, so early that it was only barely light outside. Listening, she didn't hear anything that should alarm her, and yet, her chest was aching. Getting up, and throwing on some clothes, she went downstairs to check things out.

Since the night before was Rosie's night off, another hospice nurse, named Ester was there. As soon as Hannah entered her father's room, Ester looked up. Hannah knew, in that very instant, that her reprieve had ended. "How is he?" She asked Ester as she neared her father's bed.

Wrapping her stethoscope around her neck, Ester smiled down at Frank, who had his eyes closed, and motioned for Hannah to follow her out into the hall.

They were just outside the door, and Ester left it open in case Frank made a noise and she needed to go back in.

"What's going on?" Hannah asked the nurse.

Ester smiled, but it was not a smile that reassured, it was a smile that said, 'I know this will be difficult.' She placed her hand on Hannah's arm and said, "About an hour ago, his lungs started filling up with fluid." She squeezed Hannah's arm, "I think he's tired now and is ready to let go."

Tears started to fall down Hannah's cheeks. It didn't matter that she knew this was the inevitable outcome of her father's illness, it wasn't something she was ready to hear. Instead of answering, Hannah simply nodded to Ester, and turned to go upstairs.

After knocking lightly on her parents' bedroom door, Hannah opened it and saw that her aunt was still sleeping. "Aunt Ruth," Hannah whispered.

Ruth jolted upright in bed, she tried to be ready in case she was needed to help her brother. As the sleep fog left her eyes, she saw Hannah standing in the doorway, with tears on her cheeks. It wasn't difficult to know why her niece was here. She opened her arms, and motioned for Hannah to come in.

Hannah ran to her aunt's side and jumped into the bed next to her. She allowed her aunt to hold her for a bit, rocking and running her fingers down her hair. "Ester said it's almost time," She whispered a few minutes later.

Not able to speak herself, Ruth only nodded and kissed her niece's forehead. "Well, then, I guess we'll just have to get up and get pretty so he sees us at our best."

Smiling at her aunt's perspective, Hannah realized that the idea did have merit. Her father shouldn't see them in their pajamas and looking maudlin. "Okay," She answered, and got up to go into her own bathroom.

Hannah jumped in the shower after piling her hair high up on her head. She would quickly wash up and get dressed.

Half an hour later, Hannah came out of her room, quickly followed by her aunt. They both weren't glamorous by any means, but they were dressed and had their hair done up nicely. Makeup was pointless so they started downstairs, hand in hand.

Chris was just coming in the front door when they reached the bottom landing. He only smiled and nodded his encouragement.

"I'm assuming Ester called you?" Hannah asked him.

Nodding again, Chris answered, "About an hour ago. I wanted to be here."

Reaching out, Hannah squeezed his hand in thanks and they all three went through the living room, and down the hallway toward the den.

As soon as Hannah entered the room, she felt the shift in atmosphere. It was like a tightly wound rope spanned the room, ready to snap at any minute. Ester was by her father's bedside, and listening to his lungs again. She smiled when she noticed Chris come up to the other side of the bed.

Ruth was to Chris's right, reaching down and holding her brother's hand. He opened his eyes and looked at her. She smiled and joked, "Well, look who's up so early and causing a ruckus."

Frank tried to speak, but it was too difficult. He felt as if there were a whole herd of elephants on his chest, pressing down on him. He couldn't seem to catch his breath, but he could smile at his sweet sister. Opening his mouth, he managed to get the sound "Ha," out.

As soon as Hannah heard her father, she rushed over to where Ester had just vacated. She sat in the chair, and took her dad's hand into her own. "Hi, Dad," She said softly.

He squeezed her hand, "I lu ya," he managed to get out.

"I love you too, Daddy," Hannah said, the emotion closing up her throat. She looked up at her aunt, then back down to her father, and said, "Aunt Ruth and I are here and we're going to make sure that you get up to see Mom now." The tears were flowing uncontrollably now. "I know you're tired, and I know Mom is waiting for you to be with her. I'm sure," She stopped, trying to fight back the tears, "I'm sure, she's waiting, her arms open, just for you."

Ruth was crying, her niece was trying so hard to be strong for Frank and it was gut-wrenching to see it.

Frank muttered, "Sa her."

Surprised, Hannah asked him, "You saw Mom?"

Nodding, Frank smiled, and mumbled, "Prit."

Ruth offered, "She looked so pretty, didn't she?"

Still smiling, Frank nodded. His breathing started to become shallower, his chest barely moving. He laid there, one hand holding on to his daughter's and other hand holding his sister's.

Hannah had no idea how long they sat there, the three of them, just holding hands and waiting. What surprised her was how peaceful the room felt. She saw her father's eyes widen, as if he'd seen someone he knew. Even before she looked to the end of the bed, she knew she wouldn't see anyone, but she looked anyway. Sure enough, it was only the three of them. Ester and Chris stepped out to give them privacy.

In the final minutes of her father's life, Hannah could feel a warmth on her shoulder, and knew, in her heart, that her mother was there, waiting for Frank and Hannah to both just let go.

Leaning over, Hannah kissed her father's forehead, and whispered, "It's okay Daddy, I love you, say hi to Mom and Grandma and Grandpa for me."

Ruth, allowing her own pain to show for the first time, told him, "Tell Mom and Dad they'll have to wait a while longer for me, but I'll catch up, don't you worry."

Hannah giggled at the words her aunt spoke, as usual, Aunt Ruth could find the silver lining of every cloud.

Within a minute or so, her father stopped breathing altogether. His hands went limp, his face softened, and he looked as though he wore a hint of smile on his face.

Hannah called out, "Chris, Ester?"

The two nurses came in, checked for Frank's pulse, and listened to his chest, and they both shook their heads before Chris told Hannah and Ruth, "He's gone."

And those two words would turn Hannah's world upside down.

Ruth started sobbing, with Ester trying to comfort her. Hannah just sat there, brushing her thumb across the back of her father's hand, feeling the heat slowly leave his body.

Chris leaned over to her, and said, "We would like to clean him up a bit before we make the calls," he rubbed her shoulder, "Is there anyone you would like to call to say goodbye?"

Looking over at her aunt, the question in her eyes, Hannah couldn't speak. When her aunt shook her head no, Hannah looked up at Chris and whispered, "No, thank you."

Chapter 3

Four days later, Hannah's nightmare was made a reality. She walked into the funeral home, was greeted by one of the staff members in charge of her father's service, and was shone into the room where his viewing would be held. Her aunt, uncle, and cousin hadn't arrived yet, so Hannah was on her own for the moment.

The staff member asked her, "Would you like to wait for the rest of your family, or would you like to go in and see him?"

Debating, Hannah sighed. She looked at the man, and gave him a nod, before saying, "I'd like to see him by myself."

They walked through heavy wooden doors and, even though he was across the room, Hannah's tears started flowing.

Slowly, she made her way up to where her father's casket was. The pain in her chest was magnified with every step because it was all so real now. There he was, in his best suit, looking peaceful, and here she was, all alone.

Hannah stood there for a bit, and looked down at him. She reached over and laid her hand on her father's. It was nothing like it was just days earlier, it was cold and felt waxy now. Not that it mattered really, his pain was gone, and Hannah had to hold on to that thought or she felt as if she'd just waste away with her parents. "I'm sorry you had to go," She said to her dad, "but I know you're with mom, and so happy." The tears ran down her cheeks, making her vision blurry. "I'll be fine, I don't know when, but I promise you, I'll be fine."

"That's all he wanted," Said a voice from behind her.

Turning around, Hannah saw her Aunt Ruth, Uncle Ron, and Cousin Ricky standing there. She crossed the feet that separated her from them and was glad to be held in her aunt's arms.

The four of them walked over to where her dad laid, and just looked at him. She wondered why people did that. Was it because they needed the visual reassurances that their loved one was gone? Maybe it was the need to memorize the last picture in their mind. She didn't know, and the absurdity of the question had her getting herself worked up.

Ruth was watching her niece closely, and offered, "Why don't you step out and get a breath of fresh air," she nodded towards the doors to the parlor, "the visitors will start coming in within the next fifteen minutes and you'll need all your strength."

Hannah knew her aunt was right, and she did need to compose herself, "Okay," she responded, and allowed the staff member to show her out a side door.

Thankfully, no one was out on this side of the building so Hannah had a few minutes of privacy. She was relieved that she'd taken those few minutes with her dad. It was important that she felt closure. Logically, she knew all of this, emotionally, however, was a whole different story. She'd been unable to eat more than a bite or two of food here and there, nothing held appeal for her, and she refused any visitors.

Ricky poked his head out the door, and nodded to his cousin, "Hannah," he said softly, "Mom asked me to ask you to come on back inside."

Taking one last, deep breath, Hannah nodded in return and followed her cousin back inside the funeral home.

An hour later, she was ready to bolt! There were a seemingly endless stream of "We're sorry's," and "What a tremendous loss," from people. She sat there, stiff, and lifted her hand on cue, accepting small hugs, and nodding to the words, but Hannah was tired and frustrated.

A man she didn't recognize came up to her, and took her hand into his, before saying, "Your dad was the best coach I ever had."

For the first time, Hannah smiled. Her father was a retired teacher and baseball coach for the local high school. He always told her he wanted to teach because he wasn't good enough for the big leagues but maybe he'd have the chance to coach someone who was. "Thank you," She said to the man, and watched him move on.

There were many more of those types of comments, and Hannah felt herself change during the next couple of hours. Instead of focusing on her personal grief, her mindset started to slowly turn to one of honoring her father's legacy. She'd been so busy, "taking care" of him, that she'd forgotten how many people he'd taken care of during his lifetime. One woman came up to her and told her how her father was the only teacher to listen to her when she was struggling in school and it was discovered, in large part to his efforts, that she was dyslexic. She was now a doctor.

Knowing that he'd made such an impact on others' lives soothed a bit of the pain in Hannah's heart. Before now, she only saw her father as the guy who was off of work when she was off of school, not the man who made a difference.

The Pastor from the church her parents attended came up and asked, "Are we ready to begin?"

Ruth looked at her niece, who hadn't even acknowledged the question since she was lost in thought, and nodded to him.

Hannah came out of her thought fog when the Pastor started speaking, "Can we have everyone find a seat please?" He asked. She looked around and saw that so many people had come, that there were no seats left. Another testament to her father's life and the difference he made.

The Pastor spoke, "Frank Whitman was a simple man, but a loving one….."

Smiling, Hannah looked over at her father, and knew that he was in a better place now. Silently saying a prayer that she would hold onto that faith in the coming weeks and months, she opened her eyes to see the Pastor announce, "If there is anyone who would like to say something, please come up."

For the next hour, person after person came up to say what her dad did for them. Hannah was now crying for a whole different reason. When the last person spoke, and took their seat, the Pastor announced, "Frank's family would appreciate it if you would form the procession to the final resting place…"

Her aunt cupped her elbow, and helped her get up. Securely tucked into her aunt's side, Hannah walked out with her family to a waiting car.

The ride to the cemetery took about twenty minutes. Her father wanted to be next to her mother so it was a punch to the gut for Hannah, seeing her mother's stone and knowing her father would be there too.

Almost everyone from the funeral home came to the cemetery so the parking area was full and the lane leading through the grounds was jam-packed with vehicles.

Hannah looked around, startled by the support of those who knew her father.

Her uncle and cousin were two of the pall bearers, three more were members of her parents' church congregation, and Chris, her father's male hospice nurse, was the last one.

The service at the burial site was short, but no less emotional. She sat down on a folding chair, with her aunt next to her. The Pastor's wife was on the other side of her, offering comfort, but Hannah sat there, stone-faced. Nothing they could say or do would bring her father back and Hannah wouldn't want him to suffer anyway.

As the crowd dispersed, Hannah stayed sitting there. She wasn't quite ready to say goodbye just yet. Her aunt told her, "Sweetie, it's time to go," but she didn't move.

Chris came over after the service and said to Ruth, "I'll stay with her and make sure she gets to the church for the reception."

Nodding, Ruth got up, squeezed Hannah's shoulder, and left to meet her husband and son.

Sitting down next to Hannah, Chris didn't say anything. He only sat there, offering silent support.

Hannah wasn't sure how much time had passed, but she could see the cemetery workers coming over to lower her father's casket into the grave.

Chris turned to her, and asked, "Are you sure you want to see this?"

Finally, Hannah seemed to wake up, and looked over at him, replying, "No, I don't think so."

He stood, and held out his hand for her to take.

They walked over to his car and he helped get Hannah inside before going around to the driver's side.

During the drive to the church, Hannah turned to face Chris, and told him, "Thank you, for all you did for my dad, and what you did for our family today."

Chris was feeling emotional, so only gave her a tight nod. He didn't normally become so involved with his patients, or their families, but Frank was different. He spoke non-stop about his family, his worries about Hannah after he was gone, and his late wife. Chris had the impression that Frank was torn between staying for his daughter, and being with the woman he loved. Whatever the fates brought, Chris believed that faith was tested, but Frank's never wavered. He wasn't sure he could say the same for Hannah, but he promised Frank he'd help take care of his daughter.

They pulled into the church parking lot, and Hannah saw that it too, was filled with cars. She'd been relieved when the ladies church auxiliary offered to host the reception after the service. Hannah knew she and her aunt were in no state to host such an event.

As they came down the stairs, Hannah was greeted by yet more people who spoke about her father, and the kind man he was.

By the time Hannah reached the table where her family was sitting, she was smiling, genuinely, at the people who came. Reaching down, she hugged her aunt Ruth from behind, and whispered, "Thank you," into her ear.

Ruth, surprised by the gesture, turned slightly when her niece sat down. "For what?" She asked Hannah.

"For being the best sister to my dad, and supporting me this last week," Hannah answered her.

Astounded by the change in Hannah's whole demeanor, Ruth could only stare at her niece, and mutter, "You're welcome, sweetie."

Someone brought over a plate with food piled onto it, and set it down in front of Hannah. She smiled her thanks and said a quick prayer before eating a little bit of it. Her appetite hadn't returned fully, but she realized that neither of her parents would want her to make herself sick from grief.

The afternoon passed by in a flurry. People started trickling out and Hannah waited with her family so they could personally say goodbye to everyone before they left and thank them once again.

One of the ladies from the church came over and handed Hannah a bag. It contained all the cards that people gave the funeral home and the church for her family.

Ruth looked at the large bag and asked Hannah, "Do you want me to take care of the thank you notes?"

Shaking her head no, Hannah replied, "No, I'll do it. I need something to keep my mind preoccupied until I figure out what to do."

Taking her niece to the side, Ruth said softly, "He told me about some money he had set aside for you. It's in the top drawer of his dresser, sock drawer to be exact," she smiled, and added, "He wasn't too original to be sure."

All evidence to the contrary, to Hannah's way of thinking. "I'll check when I get home," She told her aunt.

They hugged again, and Ruth wondered when they would see their niece again. With Frank gone, Ruth worried that Hannah would be lost and wither. For some reason, seeing Hannah after she came back from the cemetery, Ruth revised her earlier thought and was somewhat convinced that her niece would come around.

After saying goodbye to her family, Hannah allowed Chris to take her back to the house.

"Are you okay to go in alone?" Chris asked her when he pulled into the driveway.

Hannah nodded, and replied, "Yes, I am." She meant it too.

Chris smiled, "It was a pleasure to get to know you Hannah," he said and squeezed her hand, "I'll see you soon, okay?"

Returning his smile, Hannah answered, "It was a pleasure to meet you Chris, stay safe."

She waited for Chris to pull out of the driveway before going inside the house.

The living room was dark because the front curtains were closed. Feeling edgy, Hannah put down the bag of cards and her purse before pulling them open. The light that shown into the room was like the light that poured into her heart, it made her feel freer.

Hannah opened up the windows and decided the whole house could probably use a good airing out. She went from room to room, opening up windows and letting in the spring air.

The house felt different now, it wasn't just a makeshift hospital for her father anymore; now it was her childhood home, full of beautiful memories.

Chris arranged for her father's medical equipment and hospital bed to be taken out the day before, so now the den was once again empty.

Since she was now upstairs, Hannah went into her room to change out of her nice clothes. She put on some old shorts and college t-shirt and set to putting the house to rights.

Hours later, and after paying the neighbor boy twenty dollars to help her move the desk downstairs, Hannah felt better. It wasn't that she wanted to erase the memories of her father, she just preferred to let go of the memories of her father when he was ill.

Remembering what her aunt said, Hannah went into her parents' room. She walked over to her father's dresser and looked into the drawers but didn't find anything. She ran her hand around the edges of his "sock drawer" and realized the bottom was false. After emptying it, she managed to push up the inserted piece and, sure enough, there was an envelope.

Pulling it out, Hannah opened it to find it full of money. She didn't count it, but guessed there had to be several thousand dollars in there.

Hannah smiled, because her dad was always looking out for her.

When he'd become sick, Frank insisted that Hannah be put on all of his accounts so that, when the time came, she would be able to have access to any necessary money. The house was paid off, as was his car, so there were very few debts.

With tears in her eyes at the gesture, Hannah went back downstairs to get the bag of condolence cards from the living room.

As she walked into the newly put together den, Hannah put the bag down on the desk, and started rifling through the drawers to find a pen and paper. The funeral home supplied them with thank you notes and the sign in book, so she only had to take account of who attended and who gave a card in order to keep it all organized.

She was grabbing a pad of paper out of the bottom drawer of the desk when she saw an envelope marked, "When I'm Gone," on it. Curious, Hannah pulled out the envelope and opened it up to take out the contents.

For some reason, Hannah and her father NEVER discussed finances. She knew what bills to pay and knew that the money came out of a checking account, but they'd never discussed where the money came from. Some of it was her mother's Social Security money, as the first paper documented. Most of the money, however, came from a life insurance policy her parents took out when Hannah was only a little girl. They'd paid the premiums for years and then when her mother died, her father received the money. Her eyes wide from shock, she saw the amount was half a million dollars.

Between the life insurance and her father's disability benefits from being a teacher for so many years, he had little in the way of medical bills. It was a Blessing; Hannah knew from speaking with other people who also had sick relatives.

She came to the last papers and saw that one of them was a note from her father:

Hannah:

Your mother knew that we wanted you to be taken care of in the event that we had to leave you. I was so thankful for our forethought when your mother passed away and I became sick. There is a separate account, the paper is with the other statements, and it contains your college savings. We were smart, and put away enough for you to go after high school. Since you put your life on hold to help me continue mine for as long as possible, the money has just been building interest. Please go back to school and be the person you want to be.

I love you,

Dad

Hannah shook her head, only her father would be that wonderful!

It was so overwhelming, to think that her parents could be so concerned about something that seemed, at least at the time, unthinkable. Tears streamed down her cheeks, she felt so Blessed to have such great parents.

Chapter 4

Sitting in the office, Hannah put aside the financial papers for now. Once she figured it all out, then she would proceed, but right now, all the details seemed too much to take in.

Hannah sat back in the chair. She'd put the desk in the room so it faced the window now, and allowed her to see the neighborhood kids riding bikes up and down the street. It all seemed so normal to them, just another day of playing, while for Hannah, it was a day that would change everything from here on out.

She picked up the bag with cards and pulled them out, creating two piles on the left side of the desk. Arranging the paper and pen so she would be able to easily record who gave the cards, Hannah felt ready to do this.

Most of the cards were sweet, and people felt the need to give the gift of money. Hannah felt uncomfortable with that for some reason. She kept a detailed accounting of the money given, thinking she would just donate it back to the church, or to the high school where her father worked. Maybe they needed new practice equipment for their baseball teams? She thought her dad would certainly like that.

Almost to the bottom of the second pile of cards, Hannah opened up a solid cream envelope. It didn't feel like a card; it was too thick.

As she pulled out the contents, she noticed it wasn't a card, but an invitation. Hannah turned the envelope over but there was no return address or name on it. She turned it back over and read the invitation:

Danette Fogarty

This invitation is issued to Ms. Hannah Whitman.

In this difficult time, you have been invited to spend a week in Galveston, Texas to help you recuperate.

You will meet others who have also suffered loss.

Please contact Ms. Willa Hanson at

713-555-2245

Hannah re-read the invitation a few more times, not believing what it said at first. The invitation itself was a mystery. Should she trust an anonymous invitation to some place in Galveston? Leaning back in her chair, Hannah wondered if she really had anything to lose. She could at least call the number and speak to this Ms. Hanson to see what the circumstances were. If it seemed iffy in the least, she could just politely decline.

Before she chickened out, Hannah quickly went into the kitchen and retrieved her phone from the counter. She dialed the number and waited. A voice picked up and asked, "Thank you for calling Galveston Retreat, this is Willa, how may I help you?"

"Uh," Hannah muttered, "My name is Hannah Whitman and I received an invitation?" She asked rather than stated.

Smiling, Willa replied, "Yes, Ms. Whitman, we were expecting to hear from you."

Still unsure about this, Hannah asked the woman, "When am I supposed to arrive?"

Rustling through paperwork, Willa looked up the information for Hannah Whitman. "It says here that the reservation is set for whenever you can come."

This all seemed a little strange. "I don't know who gave me the invitation," She told Ms. Hanson.

Willa answered, "Yes, the reservations are made anonymously. Basically, someone donates the time for you."

"Can I call you tomorrow and set up dates then?" Hannah inquired.

Smiling again, Willa replied, "Sure, whenever you're ready, Ms. Whitman."

They hung up, and Hannah leaned against the counter in the kitchen and wondered if this was legitimate. She went back into the den and fired up her laptop. She'd brought it downstairs when she set up the den earlier. She put in "Galveston Retreat" and waited.

For the next half hour, Hannah read reviews about the B&B located on the island. It was an actual place, but there were no rates posted on the website. Just as Ms. Hanson explained, the days were donated anonymously.

Feeling like she should at least talk to someone about it, Hannah called her Aunt Ruth.

After explaining the invitation, her conversation with Ms. Hanson, and what the website said, Hannah asked her aunt, "So, what do you think?"

Ruth was in the car, heading back home with her husband and son, and told Hannah, "I think you'd be a little crazy not to take some time to get your bearings."

Her aunt just confirmed her own feelings. "I think you're right, thank you, love to you all," She said, and hung up.

The sun was going down and Hannah was absolutely spent from the craziness of the day. Yawning only confirmed her thoughts so she shut down the laptop, tucked away the cards, donations, and her lists.

After making sure the house was secured for the night, Hannah walked slowly upstairs, and went down the hall to her room.

She got ready for bed, but decided that tomorrow, after calling to confirm with Ms. Hanson, that she would see about donating some of the furniture in the house. It was time for change, and now seemed as good a time as any to start.

The next morning Hannah was up early and ready for work. She went through the rooms of the house, making lists of what she wanted to keep in the way of furniture, and what she wanted to donate. She called the local Salvation Army and gave them a list of what she wanted to donate and made arrangements for them to pick up the items within the next two days. After that, she called the number to Galveston Retreat. "Hello, Ms. Hanson, I'd like to start my week in about four days if that's okay?" She asked the woman.

Willa checked the calendar and answered, "That's just fine, there will be an overlap with two other guests, just so you know."

Since it was basically a hotel, Hannah didn't see any issue with that. She stated, "That's fine," and ended the call a few minutes later after getting directions from the caretaker.

With that being settled, Hannah set out to get as much done in the next few days that she could. She'd been blessed with the generosity of the financial gifts from friends of her father's so she called the school to find about making a donation in his name. The lady she needed to speak to, Ms. Jasper, wasn't in so Hannah just left her a message.

The rest of the day was spent going through closets and cupboards, separating what she could use and what she couldn't, or knew she wouldn't, use.

At moments, Hannah would come across a picture that made her stop. The grief wanted to sneak into her consciousness, but Hannah wanted to keep it at bay, at least for now. She kept herself so busy that she just collapsed into bed that night from exhaustion.

The next day was much the same, except that the men from the Salvation Army arrived and started moving out the furniture and clothing she donated.

When they left, a few hours later, the house was more than half empty.

She'd spoken to her father a few months earlier, when his speech was still good, and he'd asked her if she planned on keeping the house after he was gone. At the time, Hannah brushed it off and changed the subject, but now she wondered if she would.

The house was a nice one, well-kept, thanks to her father, along with neighbors and friends over the last couple of years. It was too big for just her, but it was paid off so she would be crazy to sell it right now before she decided what she was going to do.

What she did do, however, was call a local furniture place, after finding their website, and ordered a new bedroom set for the master bedroom. It would be too strange for her to sleep in her parents' bed, and she wanted a fresh start so she arranged for it to be delivered the next day. In the meantime, she went down to the nearby home improvement store and got paint for the master bedroom walls.

Her phone went off while she was prepping the room for paint. A tarp covered the floor, and the floorboards were taped off according to what the clerk at the store recommended. "Hello," Hannah said absently, her mind on the task at hand.

"Hannah," The woman said, "This is Ms. Jasper from the high school, and I just received the message about you donating funds in your father's name."

Stopping her paint prep work, Hannah stood up, walked into the hallway, and leaned against the wall. "Yes ma'am," She responded.

Ms. Jasper was trying to hold back tears, "I can't tell you how touched we are by your gift. I only worked with your dad briefly before he retired, but he was my coach in high school, and I always thought he was great."

Now Hannah was getting emotional, "Thank you," she whispered.

"I hope you'll come to our monthly meeting in a few weeks to present it," Ms. Jasper told her, "all the coaches will be there."

Hannah smiled, "That would be fine," she said, then asked "Why don't you email me the information so I can make sure to put it on my calendar?"

They spoke just long enough for Hannah to give the woman her email, then hung up. Hannah suspected that Ms. Jasper was finding it as difficult to deal with the situation as Hannah herself was. Putting that aside mentally, Hannah went back into the bedroom to get the new paint up on the walls.

Painting took significantly longer than Hannah anticipated. It was apparent that she was a novice, because she had to use a second coat just to fix the mistakes she made with the first coat. But, late in the evening, she was able to peel off the tape, pull up the tarp, and be proud of her work. She'd even given the walk-in closet a coat, just to spruce it up.

Hannah hadn't even been up an hour when the furniture delivery guys showed up with her new bedroom set, the next morning. She was standing in the doorway of the room, a cup of coffee in her hands, and watched them assemble the bed and put the dresser where she instructed.

With the new furniture in the room, it was time to clear out her old bedroom. "Fresh starts," She kept telling herself, as if hearing it out loud would help her keep going.

Hours later, she'd packed up all of the things that reminded her of her childhood, labeled the boxes, and tucked them up into the attic space. Her new bedroom was about Hannah, the adult, now.

She slept in her new room and felt like she was literally sweeping out the past in her life. It made her feel unsteady, but she was sure that it was the right thing to do.

Chris called her the next day, just to check in, and asked her, "How are you?"

Hannah proceeded to start telling him about everything she'd done in the last couple of days. But, instead of supporting her, Chris seemed mad.

"Why would you do all that?" He asked her. "What if you decide you wanted to keep some of your parents' things?"

Surprised by his attitude, Hannah shot back, "That's the point, this house has been a museum for a decade, Chris, and I don't think I should have to justify my actions to you."

Chris realized that he'd screwed up, and tried to apologize, saying, "You're right, I have no right to say anything about it."

Even though he sounded contrite, Hannah wasn't sure why he was so upset. "You don't," She countered, then softened her tone to say, "but I know that you are concerned as a friend and I appreciate it."

They hung up soon after, but Hannah felt that things weren't all that settled where Chris was concerned.

The last day before her trip to Galveston, Hannah went through the house and deep cleaned it. She also called her Aunt Ruth while she packed.

Ruth answered the phone with a bright, "Hello, sweetie."

Hannah couldn't help but think that her aunt was trying to sound chipper for her sake. "Hello," Hannah replied, "I wanted to talk to you before I left for the hotel tomorrow." The doubts snuck into her mind, and she asked, "Are you sure this is okay for me to do right now?"

Her aunt snorted, and came back with, "Hannah, every single person grieves in their own way," she sighed, and added, "your father relied so much on you that he was afraid you wouldn't know what to do after he was gone, now you've got somewhere to go and try to figure that out." She smiled, and added, "I think this is a true gift."

Her aunt was always someone who could reassure with a few words, and she did so again. "Thank you," Hannah answered, "I'll take it as a gift then, and work on it."

Hannah finished packing, checked the weather one more time, and then got the house in order to be shut up for a week. She was lucky that Galveston was only forty-five minutes away, if something didn't feel right she could easily just get into her car and come home.

That night, Hannah had a difficult time sleeping. She dreamt of her father for the first time since he passed away. It wasn't a bad dream, necessarily, but having him in it made her very leery about her emotional state.

She tossed and turned, and finally fell back to sleep sometime in the early morning.

The morning she was supposed to leave for her week-long trip, the weather was cloudy and cool. Not cold, but cooler than it had been. Was it a sign? Should she not go?

About noon, Hannah shored up her reserves and took her bags out to the car. She had one medium suitcase for clothes and a small toiletry bag. It wasn't much, but she didn't need much. She also didn't really know what to expect so kept her chosen attire casual.

The drive was easy, with traffic down the 45 freeway relatively light in the mid-day. As she crossed the bridge that led to the island, the sun came through the clouds and lit up the area with its beautiful intensity.

Hannah sighed in relief. Maybe this was how it was supposed to be, clouds before the sun.

She followed Ms. Hanson's directions and drove down a lane off the main thoroughfare. She was going towards the southern end of the island and had never known about this particular area. It was a string of large houses, hidden away behind a grove of trees. If you didn't know where you were going, you would miss the road altogether.

When Hannah came upon the address Ms. Hanson had given her, she put the car in park and stared.

Before her was a tremendously large Victorian home with a small sign that read, Galveston Retreat. It was painted a muted yellow, with dark green shutters surrounding the windows.

When she gained her wits about her, Hannah pulled the car into a small graveled parking area, and turned off the engine.

Before she could even get out of the vehicle, she noticed a short, round woman coming out of the front door. Her face was aged, but held a smile that made Hannah feel welcomed.

Chapter 5

"Hello," Willa Hanson called out to the young woman she presumed to be Hannah Whitman. She'd been watching for Hannah's car for some time now.

She watched closely as the new guest got out of her car. She was thin, Willa noted to herself, and she was pale. Hopefully a little beach and sun would be helpful during this time.

Hannah got her bags out of the back seat and walked up to the front porch of the big house. Her first impression was right, Ms. Hanson looked so welcoming, standing there, her apron wrapped around her waist. "Hello," She said and stopped as she reached the porch.

Willa stepped forward and wrapped Hannah into a tight hug. "Welcome to Galveston Retreat," She said quietly into the young woman's ear.

Not knowing how to respond since her bags were in her hands, Hannah leaned in slightly to acknowledge the hug, then stepped back again, and smiled. "Thank you," She responded.

Grabbing the larger of the two bags Hannah held, Willa turned to go inside, and threw a "Follow me," over her shoulder.

They walked inside and Hannah was shocked. It was amazing! The house, was even larger on the inside, than it appeared to be on the outside. The foyer was wide, with a large buffet table to one side. It held a vase with a huge spray of blooming flowers. Just breathing in the aroma from the blossoms made Hannah smile.

Danette Fogarty

Past the foyer was the main living area and it seemed to go on for ages. A huge fireplace was in the corner. The walls were done in a light tan, almost sandy color while the furniture was different patterns of neutral tones mixed with white. The part that was so intriguing to Hannah was that the color was done as if it was just thrown into the room. A vivid picture of the ocean at sunset was on one wall, while on a big, overstuffed chair, sat a brightly patterned throw pillow. All the wood was rich and dark. The floor was done in wood as well.

"Spectacular, isn't it?" Willa asked as they made their way to the staircase. "I never tire of walking into this room, it's like sunrise and sunset all at once."

Hannah thought the woman's opinion was spot on, and nodded. She followed Ms. Hanson as if she were a baby duck running after her mama.

They made their way upstairs, and came to a long corridor flanked with doors on each side. Willa told her, "Since you're the first to arrive, you get first pick."

The doors were all closed so Hannah wasn't sure what to say at first, then she turned to Ms. Hanson and asked, "Are there any rooms with balconies?"

A big smile floated across Willa's face, and she answered, "As a matter of fact, there are." She walked to the end of the hall and opened a door.

If Hannah thought the lower level of the house was awesome, the bedroom she'd just entered left her breathless. It was blues, top to bottom. The walls were done in a textured wallpaper with a blue and white flower pattern. It might've looked busy in another setting, but here, it looked whimsical. The ceiling was a sky blue. The four-poster bed had a light blue coverlet, dotted with white flowers as well. There were varying shades of the color added as throw pillows.

The vanity matched the bed in wood color and design, as did the dresser. There was a big chair tucked in the corner with a dainty table and lamp next to it. But all of that, was just a precursor to the view. There was a set of white framed French doors that opened up onto a balcony that was about 6 feet square. Not very large, but the view, oh the view was magnificent.

The house set up on a rise, probably to protect from rising Gulf waters in the event of a storm. The back yard stretched out about one hundred feet of lush, green grass, then dropped off into a hill that led down to the beach. With the sun high in the sky, the sunlight danced on the water, making it shimmer like jewels. "Wow," Hannah breathed out.

Smiling, Willa joined her, "I know, it's magical."

Turning to face Ms. Hanson, Hannah was surprised at her choice of words. Beautiful, breathtaking, magnificent, were all appropriate words, but magical……well that one word meant so much more.

"I'll leave you to unpack then," Willa told Hannah. "I'll be down to set out sweet tea and a little afternoon snack. Dinner is promptly at six o'clock so don't be late." She leaned over and hugged Hannah quickly before leaving the room.

Standing out on the balcony, Hannah watched Ms. Hanson leave, and then turned back around to once again look at the sight before her.

She didn't know how long she stood there, looking out across the constantly moving waves, but she was getting very warm. When she went inside, Hannah made quick work of putting her things away in the dresser and hanging up what she wanted to keep from getting wrinkled, in the closet. She walked over to the bed and sat on it for a minute, to test it. It was soft and Hannah had to fight back the girlish wish to jump on it as if she were eight years old again.

Stifling a giggle, Hannah cocked her head when she heard people in the hallway. The door was closed, so she couldn't see who it was, but she still walked over and listened at the door.

It was easy to hear Ms. Hanson, her voice carried down the hallway, but the other voice she had a hard time deciphering.

Sighing, Hannah decided there was time to go for a walk on the beach before dinner. Her appetite still hadn't returned fully so she wasn't sure an afternoon treat would tempt her.

After she found her bathing suit, Hannah put on a cover up, grabbed her flip flops, and headed out the door of her room.

She was closing the door behind her when she noticed a sign up on it that said, "Hannah." When she was two doors down from her room, she noticed another sign that said, "Shelby." That must be the other person she heard earlier. Not wanting to disturb the other guest, Hannah continued downstairs and found her way to the kitchen. Ms. Hanson was busy making tea and putting out cookies on a large platter.

Willa turned around, and almost dropped the plate of cookies. "Dear," She said, her eyes wide, "you startled me."

"I'm sorry," Hannah returned, "I was on my way down to the beach for a walk," she eyed up the cookies but didn't say anything.

Shaking her head, because Willa knew what the girl wanted, she held out the tray, "Take one for the road," she said and laughed as Hannah grabbed two and practically ran out the door, Willa's laughter following her as she went.

Hannah followed the path down to the beach. This part of it was practically deserted and Hannah wondered why, until she came up on gate that held a sign saying, "Private Beach, residents only."

Walking around the long gate, Hannah just kept walking down the length of the beach.

Within fifteen minutes, she was amongst throngs of people, all enjoying the summer vacation and warm weather. Kids were running in and out of the shallow water, while their mothers chatted on shore, and yelled at them periodically to be careful. There were teenagers laying out, determined to soak up as much of the sun into their skin as possible. They made Hannah think of her college days and sigh. That was in the past though. She already repeated, 'No regrets' to herself mentally about a hundred times.

Down the beach, the crowds thinned a little, just before the pier that held the local amusement park. Hannah slowed her pace and tried to scout out a place to sit for a while.

Out of the corner of her eye, Hannah happened to see a man and a little girl, crouched down just up the beach. The little girl's tone was excited, and she asked, "Can we keep it?"

Curious, Hannah made her way toward them. She heard the man say, "No, honey we can't," before she saw what they were looking at. Without thinking she crouched down beside them and said, "That's a Caretta caretta," she looked at their confused faces, and added, "It's a baby Loggerhead turtle."

The little girl's eyes widened, and she asked again, "Can we keep it, Daddy?"

It was clear to Hannah that the man didn't want to say yes, but he struggled with the inevitable anger or pouting a girl this age would undoubtedly give him. Trying to sound authoritative, she looked at the pair, and told them, "You actually can't keep him, I'm sorry, because he's an endangered species."

The man gave her a look of thanks, and then turned to his daughter to say, "Skyler, you see, the lady explained that we can't keep it."

Hannah's heart ached for the look of disappointment the little girl's face morphed into. "You know what, Skyler," she thought using her name would soften the news, and asked, "Would you like to save him?"

Both of them looked at her, not knowing what she was saying. She smiled, and informed them, "You see, there's a place you can take the turtle, where scientists who save them can nurse them and make sure they get back to the ocean and aren't hurt."

Skyler's face lit up, "Daddy," she said to her father in a serious tone, "We have to save him!"

The man nodded, "Okay, we'll save him," he looked to the young woman who stood next to him now. She was beautiful, her long hair flowing in the beach breezes. He was a good eight to ten inches taller than her, so he was looking down, but she glowed in the afternoon sunlight. "Uh," He stammered, trying to find his voice, "What do we do?" He finally got his brain cleared enough to ask her.

Her hand cupped over her eyes, Hannah looked up at the tall man and her heart flipped right in her chest. His dark brown eyes bore into her lighter gray ones and she couldn't look away. It took her about ten seconds to get her brain to answer his question. Shaking off her reaction to the man, she leaned down toward the little girl, and asked her, "Do you have a bucket or something we can carry him in?"

The little girl ran over to a pile of toys and came back with a bucket, silently holding it up for Hannah.

Smiling, Hannah took the bucket and crouched back down. She scooped just a bit of the sand into the bucket, then went over to where the waves were coming to the shore, and put just a little bit of water in the bucket, to keep the sand a little wet. The little girl followed her, noting all of her actions, and looking very determined. When Hannah crouched down next to the little turtle, Skyler did too. Very carefully, Hannah lifted up the turtle, and cupped it in her other hand. She inspected it briefly, to make sure there were no hooks in it, which there weren't, and she gently placed the little animal in the bucket.

Standing up, Hannah turned to Skyler's father, and asked him, "Do you have a car nearby?"

Asher Kelley nodded, "Yes, just over there," he turned to his daughter, "Let's get our stuff together Skyler so we can save the turtle."

Skyler didn't need to be told twice, she flew over to her pile of beach toys and started throwing them in the beach bag nearby.

Within minutes the three of them were packing the beach things into the car and Hannah was giving him directions, explaining, "There's an NOAA laboratory on the island that has a rehabilitation program for turtles."

Strapped into her booster seat in the back, Skyler asked Hannah, "What's NOAA?"

Smiling, Hannah turned to look at the little girl, thinking her pigtails looked adorable, and answered it's an acronym for National Oceanic and Atmospheric Administration."

Looking serious, Skyler then asked Hannah, "What's an acrinimp?"

"An a-cro-nym," Hannah annunciated slowly, "means that we use the first letters so we don't have to say those long words."

Seeming satisfied with Hannah's answer, Skyler nodded.

Asher was impressed, first with this woman's passion for the turtle, and then for her patience with his daughter. A six-year-old could test the patience of a saint with the endless questions, but she seemed confident in her answers.

They pulled up to a building about ten minutes later. It had a sign that read NOAA Laboratory, so they got out and went inside.

Asher held the door for his daughter and the "turtle rescuer" and allowed her to lead the way.

The front office wasn't very busy, so Hannah was able to walk up to the desk and tell the woman on the other side, "We found a baby Loggerhead and wanted to make sure it was safe."

After making a quick phone call, the woman nodded and took the bucket from Hannah, and told them, "We've got one of the students coming over from the lab to get him. Did you want your bucket back?" She asked them.

Hannah looked down at Skyler, who answered, "No thank you, I think he needs it more than I do right now."

The woman behind the desk smiled and took the turtle back through another door.

With Skyler in the lead, the three of them left the building.

They arrived back at the car and Asher realized he didn't know the woman's name. He got Skyler tucked into her booster seat, then said, "I'm Asher Kelley, by the way."

Smiling at him, Hannah looked over the top of the car and replied, "I'm Hannah Whitman."

He stood there, not moving, just looking at her, and countered, "Nice to meet you, Hannah Whitman."

They got back into the car, and Asher realized that he didn't know where Hannah was staying, and asked, "Can we drop you off somewhere?"

Before Hannah could answer, Skyler shouted, "Lunch, please, lunch please!"

Shaking his head at his daughter's behavior, Asher asked Hannah, "Would you like to join us for lunch?"

"Sure," Hannah answered right away, then wondered why she had.

They found a little diner along the main strip, and all sat down. Skyler ordered macaroni and cheese, while Asher and Hannah each ordered a sandwich.

Sitting across the table from the man and his daughter, Hannah could now see the familial similarities. They both had sandy, brown hair, but where Asher had brown eyes, Skyler had blue ones. She must've been staring for a bit, because when her eyes ran into his, she could see the unspoken question. "I was just noticing how much she looks like you."

Asher nodded, "She is like me in a lot of ways," he said, his voice almost sounding sad.

Skyler sat there, coloring on a paper placemat, oblivious to the adults' conversation.

Hannah, not being in a social setting for almost a decade, asked him, "Are you on vacation?"

"Yep," Asher answered, "right pip squeak, it's you and me." He smiled at his daughter, who returned the grin.

The words said more than enough. Hannah knew that "mom" wasn't in the picture, at least right now, and was thankful that he'd worded it that way. It would save her the embarrassment of asking, and him the embarrassment of explaining.

Nodding, Hannah, told Skyler, "It was just me and my dad too." She couldn't quite hide the look of sadness that crept into her features, feeling the sharp stab of grief as it entered her heart.

It wasn't Hannah's words that had Asher eyeing her closely, it was the tone, followed by the look of sadness that filled her eyes. It was obvious that Skyler didn't notice any of it, because she asked Hannah, "Where's your daddy?"

Not prepared for the question, Hannah's eyes immediately started to well with tears. She dabbed at them with her napkin, trying to hide them, and answered, "He's in Heaven."

With a nod, Skyler went back to her coloring, leaving the two adults there, just staring at one another. Asher mouthed, 'I'm sorry,' and Hannah mouthed back, 'It's fine.'

Their lunch came, and although Hannah thought she could eat, she found it difficult to do so. She mostly picked at her food, and moved it around the plate. A, still oblivious, Skyler dug into her macaroni and cheese, and Asher ate, but not very much. Hannah recognized something in his eyes, it was like he knew what she was going through.

After lunch, they walked out into the bright afternoon sun. Skyler turned to them, and asked, "Can we go back to the beach?"

Asher looked at Hannah and asked, "Shall we?"

She nodded.

There was no need to get back into the car, since Asher parked along the beach side of the highway before they went to lunch. They stopped at the car long enough to get out the towels and toys, and tromped down the steps to the beach.

Hannah concluded that Skyler was a professional beach goer because she knew exactly how she wanted all of her toys placed around her. She smiled at Asher as they sat down in the sand a few feet away, and commented, "She knows what she wants and how she wants it."

Asher sat down beside Hannah in the sand, they weren't touching but he felt as if there was a kind of awareness between them. It was as if they were afraid of contact. Her words bled through his thoughts and caused him to frown, before he replied, "She gets that from her mother," in a not-so-casual tone.

His words made Hannah feel as though she hit a nerve so she didn't say anything for a while.

Danette Fogarty

Chapter 6

Skyler played as Asher and Hannah watched her in silence.

Any other time, Hannah would've been uncomfortable without the conversation, but now, she was content to sit and listen to the waves. That, along with Skyler's chatter, made the time seem to fly by.

After a while, when her curiosity got the better of her, Hannah asked Asher, "Skyler is such an unusual name, may I ask how she got it?"

Without hesitating, Asher answered, "Her mother picked it out. She was always traveling and told me that her life was in the sky so she came up with Skyler."

Hannah nodded in appreciation. She'd always wanted to travel. Her parents had taken her to historic places in Texas over the summer vacations, after her father was done with baseball training. There were other places she wanted to go, but they never went.....the thoughts made her feel sad.

Asher saw the change in Hannah, more like felt it. The easiness of their being together felt permeated with emotion. "I'm sorry if I upset you," He told her.

Smiling at him, her hand covering her eyes so she could see him clearly, she whispered, "It's okay," her voice hitched and she fought the tears.

Not caring that he barely knew here, Asher pulled her closer, and put his arm around her shoulders to hold her to his side. "You go ahead and cry," He whispered into her hair, and loved the feel of it as the wind made it dance across his skin.

For the first time, since her father's death, Hannah really let the pain come up. It was tearing her apart on the inside, and she hadn't realized it until then, when she let it bubble up and spew out of her heart. Her shoulders shook with the sobs, although she kept them quiet, not wanting to upset Skyler. She wrapped her arms around Asher's chest.

They sat there on the beach, holding one another for a long time.

Skyler came up to them a while later and asked, "Hannah, do you like my dad?"

Releasing her grip on Asher's chest, Hannah was embarrassed. "Uh," She answered, "yes, I suppose I do."

Feeling the answer was good enough, Skyler merely responded with an, "Okay," and went back to playing.

Hannah looked from the child, and then to her father, before letting out a giggle. "She's certainly curious," She commented, and wrapped her arms around her knees.

"More like nosy," Asher responded, with a chuckle of his own, "but we make it work."

Feeling a little "nosy" herself, Hannah asked him, "Can I ask you, make what work?"

The moment of truth......Asher had been asked this question, in varying forms of course, over the last year. He'd been vague in the beginning, but now, he realized, the truth was always the best route. "Her mother, Stella, works for the U.S. State Department. She traipses around the world for her career, which she decided was more important than having a husband and child to tag along."

The sting of his words was unmistakable. Hannah felt sorry for him, and his adorable daughter. Without forethought, she blurted out, "Then she's stupid!"

Hearing Hannah's candor made Asher smile. He usually came to the same conclusion about his ex-wife. "She's brilliant when it comes to her job, but you're right, she's stupid when it comes to choosing that over family."

The matter, seemingly settled, was dropped. But Hannah felt bad. She'd asked him questions but knew he had some of his own, and given her reaction, was being polite enough not to ask. Shoring up her emotional reserves, Hannah explained. "My father died last week."

Asher listened to her confession, and felt horrible. "I'm so sorry," He said.

Nodding, Hannah gave him a small smile. "People have been saying that all week. I'm not the least bit sorry in some respects," She revealed, and smiled again at the look of shock that covered his features. "Not that I'm sorry he's passed away," Even the words sounded weird, "but I'm relieved that he's no longer in pain and that he's with my mother."

Now Asher understood more about Hannah, and the aura of sadness that surrounded her. He wanted, more than anything, to comfort her. He moved closer to her and, once again, put his arm around her. She was thin, he could feel it through the thin fabric of her cover up, and he felt a deep urge to protect her. "I think…" He started to say before hearing a blood-curdling, "Daddy!" Jumping up, he ran over to where his daughter was standing by a, now demolished, sand castle.

Skyler pointed to some boys who were running down the beach, "They ruined it!" She said, tears falling down her cheeks.

Crouching down, so he was face to face with his daughter, Asher told her, "The beautiful things about sand castles is that they're easy to rebuild."

Her father's explanation soothing her hurt feelings, Skyler nodded, and smiled, before asking him, "Can you and Hannah help me build a new one?"

Looking over at Hannah, Asher answered, "I know I can, but I'm not sure Hannah wants to."

Watching the two of them, Hannah was transported, for a moment or two, back to her own childhood. Her father was always quick to soothe any supposed hurt, physical or emotional, that she told him about. His empathy and care made him the beautiful father that he was. Coming back to the present, she saw both Asher and Skyler looking at her. "I'm game if you are," She announced, and got up to join them.

Hours later, the three of them sat back on their heels, and admired their work.

This sand castle was not only huge, but it was detailed. There were four turrets, all with square cut out edges. There was a moat around it, and Asher told Skyler about the alligators that lived in the moat, making her laugh.

Hannah couldn't remember the last time she'd spent so long at the beach, and was happy. The feeling was a welcomed relief after the week she'd had, and at first there was a niggling of guilt that surrounded her heart. She sat there, looking at their creation, and felt like her father would have been proud. Even if it was only a sand castle.

Noticing the sun starting to sink lower in the horizon, Hannah asked Asher, "Do you know what time it is?"

Asher pulled out his phone, checked it, and answered, "It's 5:10."

Remembering what Ms. Hanson said about dinner being promptly at six, she announced, "I'm afraid I have to get going or I'll be late for dinner."

Skyler's face fell, "Daddy?" She turned to Asher, and asked, "Can't Hannah stay with us?"

An awkward silence fell around them. Asher was in agreement with Skyler and, personally, didn't want to say goodbye to Hannah. But, he knew, as an adult, that you couldn't always get what you wanted. "I think," He turned to his daughter to explain, "that Hannah probably wants to get home. How about if we walk her there and ask if she can hang out with us tomorrow?"

Appeased by her daddy's suggestion, Skyler turned to look at Hannah, a hopeful look on her face.

'Wow,' Hannah thought to herself, 'this little girl was going to go right ahead and steal your heart.' She smiled, and replied, "You can definitely walk me back, but I'll have to get your dad's phone number and give him mine and check with the people I'm staying with about tomorrow. Is that okay?" She asked the little girl.

After a few moments of contemplation, her hand on her chin and everything, Skyler answered, "Okay."

They quickly gathered up the toys and returned them to the car. Then, all three of them began walking down the beach toward the southern end of the island, where the beach house was.

Skyler dashed ahead of Hannah and Asher, giving them a bit of privacy to talk.

"I'm sorry she's so forward," Asher offered.

Smiling, Hannah replied, "You know, I don't mind. She's absolutely adorable, and it feels nice to be wanted."

Her words, although he was sure weren't meant to, made his chest flip. If there was something he "wanted," it was to spend more time with Hannah. "She's right though," He said in a soft voice, "we both want to see you tomorrow."

Hearing Asher's words, said low so only she could hear him, did something strange to Hannah's insides. Her breathing became shallow and her stomach did flips. "Oh," Was all she could say in return.

They made it down the beach and were standing in the sand, facing the back of the Galveston Retreat house.

"It's huge!" Skyler exclaimed.

Smiling, Hannah bent down and pointed up to a balcony on the second floor, saying, "That's my room while I'm staying here."

Still in awe of the grand, old house, Skyler nodded.

Standing up, Hannah turned to Asher, and said, "I want to thank you for today. It turned out to be such a lovely afternoon."

Looking at her, Asher commented, "If saving a baby sea turtle and building a sand castle happens to make you happy, then I'm glad."

"Actually," She returned, "it does."

With a small wave, Hannah started up toward the house. She'd just about reached the porch, when she turned around and saw Asher swing Skyler up onto his shoulders. The little girl squealed in delight and started chatting about their day. Hannah watched, as father and daughter strolled back down the beach, and wore a smile when she finally turned to go into the house.

She was met with a frazzled looking Ms. Hanson, who pointed at her, "You're lucky you're on time, I was about to send out a search party."

Hannah smiled at the sweet lady, and replied, "No need, I was saving a baby sea turtle, and helped build a giant sand castle."

Placing a baked ham onto the serving dish, Willa smiled, "Well, it sounds as if you've gone and found yourself a bit of adventure then."

Nodding, Hannah said, "Yes, ma'am," and followed up with, "I'll run up and change really quickly and meet you in the dining room.

"There are two other guests for you to meet," Willa hollered after the young woman.

Hannah bounded up the stairs, much like she did when she was a teenager, taking them two at a time. She hadn't been looking and almost ran into a woman as she turned the corner to head down the long hallway. "I'm sorry," She said breathlessly.

The woman replied, "It's fine, no harm done."

Continuing down the hall, Hannah couldn't help but think that the woman was just being polite. She looked...... haunted.

Once in her room, Hannah tossed her cover up and swimsuit onto the vanity chair, and pulled out a sundress from the closet. She ran a brush through her wind-blown hair, and pulled it back into a hair band, before applying some lip gloss. She was satisfied that she wouldn't look too ragged for dinner, and went back downstairs.

Just as Ms. Hanson told her, there were two guests already sitting at the table. Both women looked uncomfortable. Studying them, as she sat down, Hannah could see the same thing in their eyes as she saw in her own this week; grief. "Good evening," She said to them both as she sat down.

The woman to her left was small, petite, with dark brown hair and beautiful chocolate brown eyes. She could be a fashion model, to Hannah's way of thinking, although she didn't look too skinny, the way some models did, she possessed an ethereal look about her; as if she were a garden sprite or something. The woman across from her, well she was something altogether different. She was tall, lanky, and looked gaunt. Grief was a heavy veil she wore.

Wanting to break the uncomfortable silence, Hannah spoke first, "I'm Hannah," she said.

The woman to her left answered, "Hi, I'm Shelby."

Willa came into the room and looked at the three of them. Oh, they were as different as day and night, and yet, they all shared a pain that needed to be mended. "Dinner is served," She pronounced with flair.

Hannah was famished, but wanted to wait until the other three women had their food, before helping herself. She'd eaten lunch with Asher and Skyler so she knew she'd been keeping up her strength. The other two, well they looked like food was the enemy.

Willa wanted to make sure they were acquainted, so she started chatting as soon as everyone got some food on their plate. "So, has everyone met?" She asked, and not waiting for an answer, added, "Hannah arrived first this morning. She recently lost her father."

Hearing Ms. Hanson's declaration about her situation left a lump in Hannah's throat. She sat there as the other two women mumbled, "Sorry for your loss."

"I received an anonymous invitation," She offered. "I wasn't sure whether to take it or not, but a change of scenery sounded good."

Happy that Hannah was opening up, Willa continued on, and said, "Shelby here," pointing to the woman across from her, "lost her husband almost a year ago."

Now Hannah's throat was almost closed. She looked to the woman next to her, and croaked, "I'm so sorry." Receiving a quiet look of acknowledgement, Hannah turned back to her own plate, but just stared at the food.

This part, although difficult, had to be done. Willa then said, "And this is Payton, her little girl passed away a few months ago."

Hearing those words definitely took what was left of Hannah's appetite away from her. "Oh Lord," She said, and covered her mouth with her hand. She remembered her father telling her that there was nothing as awful as losing a child. He told her that parents were supposed to go first, so he was following the natural order of things.

The silence swirled around the four women, like a shroud of gloom. No one spoke. No one could.

Willa Hanson would never get used to the first time she introduced guests and talked about their losses. There were varying degrees of grief, she knew that, but somehow voicing them was the hardest obstacle to overcome. "Now," She announced, "you've all been asked to come here for one thing, and one thing only." All three of the women looked at her, and she replied, "You're here to start healing."

Throwing her napkin onto her plate, the woman named Payton sighed, and almost yelled, "How can you ask that?"

Hannah hadn't expected the outburst, and could only watch as the woman stood up, and looked at Ms. Hanson with a look of fear and pain, before saying, "My little girl is in the ground, and I'm supposed to just move on?" She demanded, looking at all three of them, "Maybe you can do that, but I can't!" She turned and left the room.

Knowing how much someone was hurting was bad enough, but hearing the pain tear through them was something else altogether. Willa looked at Hannah and Shelby, and said, "You will each need to get through your pain in your own way."

Nodding like an obedient child, Hannah didn't answer. Instead, her mind swam with thoughts of her parents. The happy days when she was around them, and feeling secure and loved.

That's what she chose to focus on right now. If it was hiding from the pain, then so be it.

Shelby pushed back from the table, and quietly placed her napkin beside her plate, "If you don't mind," she directed her words at Ms. Hanson, "I'd like to take a walk on the beach."

Ms. Hanson nodded to her, and sat there, watching as Shelby walked out the door. Once the back door shut, she turned to Hannah and said, "I think that went well."

Not sure what Ms. Hanson's definition of "went well" was, Hannah just stared at her.

Chapter 7

Later that night, Hannah was sitting out on the balcony when she saw Shelby walk back up toward the house. Not bothering to turn on the lights, as she preferred the solitude of the darkness, Hannah was pretty sure that the other woman didn't see her sitting on the porch. She studied Shelby, and thought she moved with a kind of gracefulness. It wasn't something natural, it was more like something she'd practiced for years, and was now part of her demeanor.

The night was quiet. Every once in a while you would hear noise drift on the breeze, from down the beach, but the quiet surrounded the house. Maybe an hour earlier, Hannah thought she heard a woman crying, and assumed it was Payton. Not knowing the woman well enough to intercede, and offer a shoulder, Hannah decided to sit out on her balcony and contemplate her own grief.

Of course, now, that included thoughts of Asher, and how he held her. The images played in her mind like a never-ending movie. The feel of his hands around her shoulders, the feel of his solid chest beneath her own fingers, and the way he soothed her. It was a little scary, since it was so easy.

Maybe Skyler was the reason? The little girl was absolutely delightful and Hannah couldn't help but consider that she felt drawn to Skyler's curious demeanor. They were both, for all intents and purposes, living without a parent.

The thought stopped Hannah in her mental tracks. She got up and walked to the railing, and leaned on it. The little girl still had her parents, both of them, whereas Hannah had neither of hers. There was little use in saying they were the same.

Danette Fogarty

Her mood turning sour, Hannah decided to try and get some sleep.

Hours later, she still lay in the bed, staring at the ceiling. Her stomach was growling since she'd barely touched her dinner, but she was too tired to get up.

The house seemed quiet, the only sounds Hannah could hear were those of the waves hitting the beach through the French doors she decided to leave open.

A noise roused her from her undemanding thoughts. Straining to hear, Hannah sat up, and waited. Sure enough, someone was moving around. Throwing the sheet off of her, Hannah decided to investigate.

Even though the house seemed old, it was solid. Hannah moved through the hallway quietly, and went downstairs. She heard another sound and went in the direction of the kitchen.

When she was at the doorway to the room, she saw Shelby sitting at the breakfast table, a glass of milk cupped between her hands, and some ham from dinner, sitting on a plate.

Hannah knew the moment Shelby became aware of her because she jumped and asked, "Oh, I'm sorry, I didn't wake you did I?"

Shaking her head no, Hannah stepped into the room, and made her way over to sit across from Shelby at the table. "No, you didn't, I heard a noise and was being nosy, but I wasn't sleeping."

"My husband, Kent, used to say that sleeping was something that didn't come naturally to me." She smiled at the memory, then her face contorted into pain.

Hannah reached across the table and held Shelby's hand. "I'm not sure if we're supposed to talk about this, but my dad died last Monday. ALS," She smiled when Shelby squeezed her hand. "He was sick for eight years."

Shelby's eyes came up and captured Hannah's. "Oh, Hannah," She said, "I'm so sorry."

The fact that this woman, who just lost her husband, was able to feel empathy, made Hannah want to break down. "If you don't mind my asking, how did your husband die?" She asked Shelby.

It took a few moments for Shelby to collect her thoughts, then she explained, "He was on his motorcycle, coming home from the gym, and a driver didn't see him and pulled out."

A tear slid down Hannah's cheek at the absolute agony that shone on Shelby's face. "I'm so sorry," She said to Shelby, "I shouldn't have asked."

Clearing her throat, Shelby replied, "You should." She looked at this woman, who she was fast considering a new friend, and offered, "I should talk about it. I haven't you know."

"Talked about it?" Hannah asked her.

Nodding, Shelby sighed. "At first, I just couldn't wrap my head around it, you know?" She looked at her glass of milk, then up again at Hannah, before saying, "And then, after the funeral, and all the "I'm sorry's" and "Such a waste's" I just wanted to hunker down and forget about it."

That part, Hannah could relate to. "My father knew he was going to die, and he did, very slowly." She tried to smile but it didn't quite reach her eyes, "It was agony, seeing him slip away, bit by bit."

"And your mother?" Shelby asked Hannah.

Giving a small smile, Hannah answered, "She passed away my sophomore year in high school."

'Dear Lord,' Shelby thought to herself. "Now I feel ashamed," She said out loud.

Shocked by Shelby's statement, Hannah asked her, "Why?" She leaned forward, "I had the best parents any kid could wish for. I'm totally pissed that they were taken away, yes, but I wouldn't change the way they were with me, or the way they were at all."

Now Shelby was astonished by Hannah's outlook. "What a wonderful way of looking at it," She told Hannah.

"Actually," Hannah told her, "it was something a man said to me at Dad's funeral."

She didn't expand on the thought, and Shelby didn't ask any more questions. They just sat there, staring into space, each lost in their own thoughts, but still feeling comfort that the other person was there.

The next morning, Hannah woke up to sunshine pouring into her room.

She had to blink to get her eyes to adjust to the brightness. Sitting up, she wondered what time it was and groped along the nightstand until her hand skimmed across her phone. Lifting the device up, she noticed it was barely 8am. She didn't know why she was up so early, but there was no going back to sleep now.

After using the bathroom, Hannah pulled her hair back, and went downstairs. She saw Shelby first, and her heart ached for the woman. "Good morning," Hannah said to her, before sitting down on a sofa across from where Shelby was sitting.

"Good morning," Shelby said to Hannah. The woman seemed nice enough, it was just that Shelby had been so anti-social since her husband's death, that she didn't remember how to be gracious. Even though she talked with Hannah the night before, it somehow seemed different in the bright light of day.

Payton came down the stairs, slowly, and joined them.

They sat there for a few minutes, each unsure of what to say. Shelby spoke first, saying, "My husband, Kent, was wonderful." She swiped at tears in her eyes, "He'd be so mad at me if he was here."

Nodding to Shelby, Hannah, smiled. "My dad, Frank, was all about me getting on with my life, and now I just feel lost."

Payton said nothing, only sat there. The other two woman allowed her this time to process, without judgment.

Willa came into the room, and was shocked by what she was witnessing. Very seldom did guests actually start talking without prompting from her. She left the room, wanting to give them a few more minutes before announcing breakfast.

"Kent taught gymnastics and was the funniest guy," Shelby offered.

Hannah chuckled, and added, "My dad always thought he was funny too, but he really wasn't."

For the first time since they'd met her, they saw Payton begin to smile.

"What did your dad do?" Payton asked Hannah.

Pleasantly surprised by Payton's participation, Hannah told her, "He was a teacher."

Both Payton and Shelby nodded their understanding, and everyone became quiet once again.

Ms. Hanson came into the room and told them that, "Breakfast is served," and they got up to follow her.

This meal was a little lighter, in Hannah's opinion anyway than the dinner the night before. The food, still wonderfully prepared and presented, was great, but the heaviness of emotion was lighter today. It was a relief in some ways, but a little disturbing in others. Hannah wasn't sure which way she was "supposed" to feel so she just ended up feeling muddled.

"What's on everyone's agenda today?" Willa asked the three women.

Payton shrugged, Shelby mentioned something about going to Moody Gardens, and Hannah piped up, saying, "I'm going to meet up with Asher and Skyler Kelley.

The other two women gave Hannah a questioning look, so Willa told them, "A father and daughter that Hannah helped out yesterday."

Not that these strangers' opinion of her really mattered, Hannah still felt a weighty hesitation inside herself at their looks.

She couldn't eat any more, preferring to push the food around her plate for the reminder of the meal.

Willa was well versed on when to call a meal quits. With people who were in the throes of grief, they were never very long, at least in the beginning. No one really cared to eat, only went through the motions to keep themselves going. "Okay, so Shelby, why don't you give me a hand in cleaning up, since Hannah was kind enough to do it last night?"

Shelby nodded, a slight smile lightening up her features. Payton excused herself and went back upstairs to her room. Hannah sat at the table for a few more minutes, staring into space.

That's where Ms. Hanson found her, and asked, "Are you going to just take up space at the table, or are you going to go out and find another adventure?"

The words made Hannah smile. She knew when she was "excused," and got up. Following Payton's lead, she went back upstairs to her room.

A few minutes later, she'd found a book that she wanted to read on one of the book shelves in her room. It was old and seemed interesting.

Going out onto the balcony, she sat down in the chair, pulled her legs up underneath her, put her sunglasses on, and started to read.

Hannah looked up from her book, sometime later, and noticed the sun was high in the sky above. She was about to get up, to go inside, when she heard her name being called. Looking over, she saw Asher, with a waving Skyler, sitting on his shoulders. Smiling, she waved back and got up to cross to the railing. "What are you two up to?" She called down to them.

Asher had come to the house where Hannah was staying at the absolute insistence of his daughter. It was like Skyler was on some mission, she was so adamant. But, then he saw Hannah, sitting up on that porch, and his stomach tightened with an anticipation he hadn't felt in years. He felt like the sand under his feet, constantly moving with the wind and water.

Skyler shouted, "We're waiting for you, Hannah, can you come with us?"

He watched Hannah's face as it changed into a wide smile, and she answered, "Yes, I'll be right down."

Hannah turned around to go into her room, the sight of Payton going back into her room out of the corner of her eye. The look she managed to see on the other woman's face was that of pure torment. Hannah couldn't deny that seeing Skyler probably brought memories of her little girl to her mind, and felt awful. She was about to rethink her decision to go, when she heard Skyler yell, "Come on, Hannah!"

Willa heard a little girl yelling, and went out the back door. 'So,' she thought to herself, 'this must be the Asher and Skyler Hannah was talking about.' "Hello," She greeted them.

When Hannah was going through the kitchen, she heard voices. A smile lifted her features when she opened the back door, and saw Ms. Hanson giving Asher and Skyler cookies. "Is she plying you with baked goods?" She asked Asher.

His mouth full of delicious cookies, Asher nodded like a little boy. Skyler lifted her cookie up to show Hannah, proud of her gift.

Willa offered a cookie to Hannah, who politely declined it, with a small shake of her head. But, there was no mistaking her happiness at seeing her new friends, and Willa was pretty sure those were sparks she saw passing between Hannah and Asher. "I'll head in to make lunch for Payton and myself," She busied herself with picking up the plate of remaining cookies, and added, "You three have fun."

Hannah waved to Ms. Hanson, and followed Asher and Skyler down the steps. As soon as they were on the grass, Skyler skipped over between the two adults, taking each of their hands into one of hers.

The three of them walked down to the beach, the adults listening to Skyler as she gabbed about a lot of things, skipping topics as easily as a smooth stone skipped across a calm lake.

They came to the area where most of the beachgoers were set up. Skyler released their hands when she saw her pile of beach toys and other kids playing.

Asher silently walked next to Hannah, and fought the urge to take her hand into his. It was easier with Skyler between them, since she made a little barrier. Now, without her, he ached to touch Hannah.

Hannah was fighting her own feelings, without any knowledge of what Asher was thinking. He seemed almost tense today. "Did I impose?" She asked him as they sat down, a few yards from where Skyler played with another little girl.

Surprised at the question, Asher answered with a hasty, "No!" Then asked her, "Why would you ask me that?"

Blowing out a breath, Hannah explained, "Well, there is something a little different today, like you're tense."

Did he tell her he was tense because she made him that way when he saw her? Did he explain to her that no one made him feel that way, not even his ex-wife? 'No!' His mind shouted to him. Instead, he told her, "I'm not sure how to be around you."

His answer left Hannah confused. "Oh," She answered, and asked him, "Is it because of my dad?"

It wasn't a lie, he did worry about her newly felt loss. "A little," He answered.

Hannah nodded. "It's weird," She started, "my dad was so worried about how I would go on after he was gone. And when he did pass away, I swept through that house like a tornado, cleaning and clearing out what I didn't need."

Asher could understand some of that, "It's a new beginning."

Smiling, Hannah told him, "It is, and I'm ready for it, probably have been for a while, but I wanted to make sure he was okay too."

He watched his daughter, as Hannah spoke, and hoped that she loved him as much as Hannah seemed to love her father. "Loss is never easy."

Remembering that he'd experienced his own loss, Hannah asked him, "Does her mother see her a lot?"

A frown planted on his face, at the memory of his ex-wife, Asher replied, "No, she hasn't seen her for almost a year."

"I can't comprehend that!" Hannah said emphatically.

Asher looked over at Hannah, his smile back, and he said, "Me either, I can't imagine being without her for any significant length of time."

Skyler ran over to where her dad and Hannah were sitting, and showed them a shell she found on the beach. When she ran back to where her new friend was, Hannah spoke up, saying, "She's simply adorable."

Nodding in agreement, Asher wondered why his ex-wife couldn't see something that an almost complete stranger could.

Chapter 8

Hannah spent the rest of the afternoon with Asher and Skyler, laughing at Skyler's haphazard attempts at swimming, and Asher pretending to rescue her.

She watched them, wondering if that was how her dad felt about her. It was a bittersweet thing, remembering and feeling as if maybe she didn't ask her father everything she should have.

As they did the previous day, Asher and Skyler walked her back to the house just before dinner.

When they reached the backyard, Skyler ran ahead of them, and knocked on the back door. They watched as Ms. Hanson invited the little girl into the kitchen.

"Thank you again, for another great day," Asher told Hannah.

She wasn't sure why he was thanking her. "No," She responded, "thank you. It was so nice to get out."

Feeling nervous, Asher shuffled his feet a little, before asking, "Hannah, I don't know how to ask this exactly, probably because it's been years, but would you go out to dinner with me?"

It had been a long time since Hannah received an invitation for a date. "Uh," She said, not really knowing what to say.

"I know, it's silly, isn't it?" Asher asked rhetorically. "I mean, you barely know me."

Hannah smiled, mostly because he was looking down at his feet as if he were a small boy who just got in trouble, and was being shy. She reached up, and lifted his chin with her fingers, and said, "I think I'd really like to go out with you, Asher."

Skyler burst through the back door just then, and ran over to where they were standing. "Are you ready, Daddy?" She asked Asher.

Asher nodded to her, and then looked up at Hannah and thought, 'Yes, I think I am,' to himself.

After dinner, Hannah helped Ms. Hanson clear the table. She felt bad that the beautifully cooked dinner was barely touched. "I'm sorry if your efforts feel wasted," She said to the caretaker.

Willa smiled, and answered, "Never wasted, I donate any food we don't use to a local shelter, but usually, it does get eaten."

Given the presentation, and obvious culinary skills Ms. Hanson possessed, Hannah believed her. "I had a good day," She said casually, as she loaded dishes into the dishwasher.

"Saving turtles and building sandcastles again?" Willa said to her, then winked.

Shaking her head no, Hannah smiled. "We just played on the beach."

The irony of the situation wasn't lost on Willa. "Oh, and where is Skyler's mother?" She asked out of sheer curiosity.

Hannah reminded herself to never misstep around Ms. Hanson. "She's off working for the State Department, and is divorced from Asher." Her words sounded strange as she spoke them.

Now Willa nodded in understanding. She did stick her nose in when it came to the people who stayed at the Retreat. She

Danette Fogarty

knew that grieving people tended to grasp onto things in order to alleviate the pain they felt and, sometimes, even walked into unhealthy situations. If a few prying questions helped keep them on the right path, then Willa was happy to ask those questions.

"Asher asked me out on a date tomorrow, I think," Hannah blurted out as she put the leftovers in the refrigerator. "I want to go."

If there was one thing Willa knew, from all her years here, was that the grieving always needed permission to live their life, at least for a while. "I think that sounds very nice," She responded.

Smiling, Hannah walked over and gave Ms. Hanson a quick hug before turning to go upstairs. "Goodnight," She said as she left the room.

A smile on her face, Willa waved a hand and sat down at her computer to send out a few emails.

Hannah got ready for bed, but didn't feel like sleeping just yet. She left the lights in the room turned off, and walked out onto the balcony. Sitting down on the chair, she lifted one leg up, and wrapped her arm around it. The night breeze was light, and felt good as it slid across her skin. She'd gotten some color from being out on the beach today, and was lucky she hadn't burned.

She was so pale these days, after being inside for most of the last two months, she couldn't remember the last time she'd been outside for that long. A picture of her father made its way into her mind. He was smiling, and Hannah closed her eyes to savor the sight of him.

A little while later, she heard a sound, and opened her eyes up again. Looking around, she found the source of the sound; it was Shelby making her way up the hill to the backyard of the house from the beach. She sat down on the grass, and faced the ocean, just as Hannah did.

There was a small sob, and Hannah looked over to her right. There, on another small balcony, sat Payton. She was holding a small blanket, and cried into the fabric.

Hannah couldn't help but think that the three of them needed to be here, now, more than any of them really thought.

The next morning, Hannah came downstairs. Shelby was sitting in the living room, reading a magazine. She still looked tired, but better than Hannah remembered her looking the day before. "Good morning," Hannah greeted her.

Looking up from her reading, Shelby answered, "Good morning."

Not sure if she should speak up or not, Hannah thought about what Ms. Hanson said the night before, and decided to comment to Shelby, "I saw you sitting out last night."

Her eyes raising to meet Hannah's, Shelby asked her, "Did I disturb you?"

Now Hannah felt awful, since Shelby looked like she'd done something wrong. "No, not at all," Hannah rushed the words, "I was sitting out on my balcony last night," she offered.

"Me too," Came a voice from the bottom of the stairs.

Both women turned to see Payton standing there.

Danette Fogarty

Hannah smiled, "I heard you," she moved over to silently offer a seat to Payton, and was surprised when the woman walked over to sit down.

Looking embarrassed, Payton, murmured, "Sorry."

Feeling sorry for the woman, Hannah grabbed her hand, and told her, "You have nothing to be sorry for, Payton, you're in pain."

Although she didn't respond, Hannah felt as if Payton appreciated her words.

"I feel better, being around the two of you," Shelby blurted out, in a kind of announcement.

Hannah looked over at the woman she thought was so graceful, and smiled. "Me too," She responded, "I don't have to make pretenses, or act strong, because the two of you feel what I feel."

Payton nodded, then added, "But I'm still so angry."

Since she was still holding Payton's hand, Hannah squeezed it again, and asked, "You know that's okay, right?"

Shaking her head no, Payton, replied, "No, I don't know what's right anymore."

The three women sat there, contemplating the weight of the words, when Ms. Hanson came into the room. She put her hands on her hips and declared, "This conversation will have to be paused, and the three of you will come into the dining room, and for Heaven's sake, will somebody eat the food I've cooked?"

Looking at Shelby, then at Payton, and finally to Ms. Hanson, Hannah started to laugh.

It took about a half a minute before Shelby joined in. Payton didn't actually laugh, but a smile formed on her face before she stood up to join the others for the meal.

Almost an hour later, Hannah felt lighter, emotionally. The food was delicious, but none of them felt like eating too much more than they had previously. There was a little more conversation, and Hannah realized she'd missed that. None of them spoke of their lost loved ones, but, as Shelby said earlier, they didn't have to. Not here, not with these other women who shared their grief. It didn't matter that their grief was different, about different people in their lives, or at different stages in their adjustments, it was just nice to feel the support of others who fully understood.

Hannah offered to help Ms. Hanson clean up after the meal, while Shelby ran to the store to pick up something she needed, and Payton retreated back to her room. Hannah chewed on her lip as she put the dishes into the dishwasher.

"You're going to chew that lip clean off, if you don't say what's on your mind," Willa said to her, a few minutes later.

Smiling, Hannah answered, "I was just thinking about what Payton said earlier."

Willa nodded, and asked, "About feeling angry?"

It shouldn't have surprised Hannah to know that the caretaker overheard their conversation, but it did. The house wasn't completely quiet, and Ms. Hanson was the one keeping an eye on them, so naturally she would hear some of the discussions by the guests. "I am upset about my dad passing away, but I'm not angry," She admitted.

Danette Fogarty

Sitting down at the kitchen table, Willa motioned for Hannah to join her. "Losing someone you love is hell, let's just face it," She stated, then added, "but losing your baby, whether the child is eighteen months, or eighteen years; is like being gutted with a melon baller."

The description gave Hannah pause. She'd never heard such words regarding grief, even when her mother passed away and her father and she were left to fend for themselves. She also had the distinct impression that Ms. Hanson wasn't just talking out of experience with the house, but that she had first-hand knowledge of the feelings. Hannah was about to ask her about it when she heard her name being called.

Willa would answer any questions the guests asked, openly and honestly, but before Hannah could ask, she heard the young woman being summoned, and smiled. "I'm guessing that's little Skyler, looking for you."

Nodding, Hannah smiled in return, "It would seem so."

Before Hannah could leave, Willa asked her, "So, have you decided that you are going to go out with the handsome Mr. Asher?"

There was no mistaking the innuendo of Ms. Hanson's tone, but Hannah felt it was harmless. She bit her lip as she tried to keep her smile at bay. "I want to, but we'll see," She answered, and got up to go outside.

Willa stood, walked to the window, and watched as Hannah darted out to where Asher and Skyler were standing on the beach. She watched as the three of them left, then went over to her computer to send out her emails.

"So," Hannah said to Skyler when she met up with them, "I guess we're not going to the beach today."

Skyler dutifully shook her head no, then answered, "Nope, Daddy is taking us to a museum."

Hannah looked up from the child, and into her father's eyes. The feeling that gave her was as if she'd just willingly stepped off a high ledge…...she fell into the depths of his eyes, and was gladly engulfed into his gaze.

Asher's face stayed neutral, but his insides were doing cartwheels. She was stunning! Those were the words that just raced around his ever-tumultuous mind. When it finally dawned on him that both Hannah, and Skyler were looking at him, he offered, "Uh, yes, we're going to the museum."

It didn't escape Hannah's notice that Asher was a little lost when he looked at her, because Hannah felt exactly the same way when her eyes met his. Instead of calling him out on it, she decided a nod would be sufficient.

They walked down the beach to where Asher parked the car, and got in. At Skyler's request, Hannah was the one who put her in the car and clicked her booster seatbelt in place. When she stepped back to close the door, her eyes, once again, stumbled right into Asher's. And again, her body was giving off signals like crazy. She rubbed her hands down the side of her skirt as she made her way back around to the passenger side of the car. Asher opened her door for her, which was a new level of sweet, to her way of thinking, and she mumbled, "Thanks," as she got into the car.

The drive into Houston was nice. Traffic was a little heavy, but the speed wasn't diminished too badly, and they found themselves finding parking for the Natural History Museum in no time. With Skyler's chatting, the time flew by in a series of questions regarding Hannah's house, her parents, and anything else the little girl could come up with. Although not used to the rigorous questions, Hannah was happy to oblige the little girl. She did notice, however, that Skyler's daddy was very quiet. Even more so than the day before, and that started to worry Hannah by the time they were making their way into the massive building. "Are you okay?" She asked Asher as they waited in line to get their tickets to enter.

Asher spent the last hour listening to all sorts of things about Hannah. One thing he discovered, was that he enjoyed the sound of her voice. Another was that she lived a pretty normal life, by all accounts. Yet another, was that he was fascinated by anything that had to do with her. "Uh, yeah," He answered her question, and looked away.

Stepping forward, since it was their turn, Hannah let it go, but she did watch him closely after that.

They walked around the museum, oohing and aahing appropriately over the exhibits. Skyler was asking more questions, that Asher patiently answered. Some were directed at Hannah, about whether she'd ever gone to the museum with her daddy. "I did," She told the little girl, "but it was years ago!"

"That must make you sad," Skyler told her, and grabbed her hand.

Trying to remember the last time she and her dad went to anything other than doctor's appointments, was tough. But, Hannah didn't want to dwell on the memories of his illness. She smiled down at Skyler, and whispered, "Sometimes, yes, but I'm just glad we got to go."

Skyler seemed very content with the answer, and looked up at Asher, before saying, "I'm glad we got to go too, daddy."

In an attempt to hide his emotions, Asher scooped up his daughter, and plopped her on his shoulders. "Me too," He answered, and cleared his throat.

Being able to witness the moment gave Hannah a mixture of happiness and sadness. She was happy to see Asher and Skyler be close, but sad that she would no longer have those moments with her own father. She imagined that this bittersweet feeling would be one she'd never quite get over. And, that was just going to have to be okay.

They walked the entire museum, and decided to go to a local restaurant nearby, afterward.

Asher managed to keep his daughter's questions for Hannah on a less emotional path, by distracting her with the museum's vast array of exhibits. He could see that Skyler's innocent questions were disturbing some memories that were probably still raw. He felt bad about it, and told Hannah, "I'm sorry about her interrogations," as they sat down.

Without thinking, Hannah put her hand on his shoulder, and replied, "It's fine; I enjoy her company."

Now it was his turn to not think, and he asked her, "Just her company?"

The look Hannah shot him was one mixed with a slight amount of confusion, and a healthy dose of awareness, "No, not just her company," she replied as he pulled out her chair and allowed her to sit.

Suddenly, everything was different. At least in Hannah's mind. His words were laced with something sharp. Whatever it was, it was making her insides turn into jelly. She literally had to put her hand to her belly, and demand her body settle down.

As Asher sat down, across from Hannah, he smiled. It was a smile of male appreciation, and he enjoyed the way it seemed to fluster the beautiful Hannah. He was attentive to his daughter, but always kept an eye on Hannah, and didn't mind that he was doing it, not one bit.

Getting through lunch, was difficult. Hannah wanted to yell at Asher to stop looking at her that way, but she couldn't. Not only would it upset Skyler, but Hannah herself actually liked the feeling his eyes gave her. It was a little intense, but what woman didn't enjoy the attention of a handsome man?

They took Hannah directly back to the bed and breakfast she was staying in, after they left the restaurant. Asher knew that Skyler would most likely pass out in the car, and she did. It gave him the opportunity to talk to Hannah about more grown up things. He asked her, "How about dinner tonight?"

Hannah couldn't think of anything she'd enjoy more, so she told him, "Yes that would be great."

Chapter 9

After Asher and Skyler dropped her off, Hannah went inside and practically floated through the rooms.

She came across Ms. Hanson first, and asked, "Hello there, how was your afternoon?"

Willa could recognize the signs of love from fifty paces. If Hannah wasn't all the way into the deep end of that emotional pool, she would be soon. It was nice to see her so happy, but a little disconcerting too, as Willa wasn't sure she was dealing with what she had to, her father's death. Instead of bursting Hannah's proverbial bubble, she asked her, "And when are you seeing the handsome Asher, again?"

"Tonight," Hannah replied, and went into the refrigerator for some bottled water. "Although," She said, a realization gripping her, "I'm not sure what clothes I brought for a dinner date."

Waving her hand, Willa assured her, "If you don't have something, I'm sure I do."

Her eyebrows raised, Hannah followed Ms. Hanson into a set of rooms that was just off the kitchen. They were obviously Ms. Hanson's private rooms, and Hannah felt a little silly that she hadn't even noticed the doorway that led to them before now.

They walked through a spacious sitting area, and into the bedroom. It wasn't too big, just enough room for a queen-sized bed, a bedside table, and a dresser. The furniture was done in a deep, rich brown, and Hannah absently ran her hand over the top of the dresser as she waited for Ms. Hanson to dig around in her closet.

While waiting, Hannah noticed a picture. It was in black and white, and was taken a long while ago, if the people's outfits were any indication.

Willa came out of the closet, a dress in her hands, and found Hannah looking at the single picture she kept in her room. She smiled fondly, as she watched Hannah look at it. "That's me, many years, and pounds ago," She told Hannah.

Smiling, Hannah picked up the picture. She ran her fingers over the image, as if doing so would bring a memory to her. "I'm guessing this is your family?" She asked Ms. Hanson.

She nodded as she walked over to where Hannah stood. Without saying anything, she gently took the picture from Hannah's hands, and also ran her fingers over the glass that covered the image. "Yes, this is my husband, Jack, and our son, James."

Hannah watched the emotions skitter across Ms. Hanson's face. There was remembrance, happiness, and sadness too.

Willa could see the questions in Hannah's eyes, and answered them with, "We lost James about fifteen years ago," she started to say as she put the picture back in its place, "and then Jack, God rest his soul, went to Heaven about five years ago." As if she was realizing something, she quietly asked, "Has it been that long?"

The feeling of being an interloper consumed Hannah. She could see the pain, still, in Ms. Hanson's eyes. "I'm sorry," She told the older woman, then cringed inwardly as the words that she herself hated to hear, just came out of her mouth.

Patting Hannah's shoulder, Willa smiled. "It's okay, I'm okay," She told her, "I just always get surprised by how quickly the time passes." She absently handed Hannah the dress she had laid over her arm, "I guess it just means that I'll be with them soon enough."

Hannah couldn't help but wonder if Ms. Hanson's words didn't reflect her own feelings, to some extent at least. There were moments, albeit few, but there still were some, when Hannah wished she could just drift away, and be with her parents. "I think the same things sometimes," She blurted out, and was shocked by her admission.

Willa, not one to be easily surprised, was. "You're so young," She said to Hannah, "surely you know that your life is really just beginning."

Plopping down on the nearby bed, Hannah sighed, then asked, "Is it?" She silently pleaded with Ms. Hanson for answers, "I want it to, sure," she said, then added, "But sometimes I wonder if I wasn't meant to be alone."

Sitting down beside Hannah, Willa gently took Hannah's hand into her own, and leaned over to whisper, "It would be nice to think so, sometimes, but we truly are never alone." As if to make her point, she looked up, her eyebrows raised.

To that end, Hannah had to agree. "I know, and I believe, but sometimes…" Her sentence drifted off.

Putting up her hand to stop any further argument, Willa told her, "No, you can't let yourself go down that road, we are never meant to be alone." She stood up and pointed to the picture on the dresser, "We're meant to live, and love, and learn the lessons that we're meant to learn, I can't accept any other explanation."

Again, Hannah agreed, it was just difficult not to be drawn into the "what ifs" and "maybes" of the world. "Is that why I'm going out on a date only a week after my father died?" She asked Ms. Hanson.

Sitting back down, Willa smiled, "It's why you're trying to find out who you are, and what you want."

Not exactly the answer Hannah hoped for, but, for now, it would have to do. She nodded in understanding, and finally looked at the dress she was handed, her face morphing into a big smile. Oh, it was beautiful! It was black, done in a soft fabric, and form fitting.

"Now, before you ask, it's not mine," Willa told her pre-emptively.

Hannah didn't ask, because she wasn't sure she'd like the answer. Instead, she just nodded, and walked over to the mirror, holding the garment in front of her.

Willa came up behind her, and said, "If it's too big, I have a scarf you can use for a belt, but I think it will be pretty good."

An hour later, Hannah was sitting on the porch, off of her room, and staring out into the Gulf. The information that Ms. Hanson gave her, along with the revelation of the older woman's own losses, made Hannah think she was maybe acting a little irrationally. Now, in the midst of her grief, she was just going to fall in love? She didn't want to use that word, but it certainly felt like it applied to her.

Thoughts of Asher, with Skyler and her, swam around her brain. How he made her feel, whenever their eyes met gave Hannah goosebumps. But even with all of that, was now the time for her to jump into a relationship? Much less, a relationship that involved a beautiful little girl? These questions weighed heavily on Hannah's mind.

She looked up, to see Payton and Shelby walking toward the house, a smile taking over where the frown of thought was. It was good to see Payton out and about. They happened to look up, and Hannah waved her greeting. Both women waved back, and that made Hannah feel better.

At seven o'clock, Hannah came downstairs. She was dressed in the dress that Ms. Hanson loaned her, and felt pretty for the first time in a long time. The dress was just a bit loose, so she borrowed the colorful scarf Ms. Hanson mentioned earlier, tying it around her small waist. Looking in the mirror, Hannah saw a person who was too skinny. She'd have to work on that.

"Oh," Willa whispered when she saw Hannah come down the stairs. She looked beautiful! She wore the dress well, the scarf making a splash of blues and greens next to the black fabric. She wore a pair of sandals that she'd brought with, and they gave a casualness to the outfit that was perfect for the island restaurants.

Just as Hannah reached the bottom step, the doorbell rang. Nerves flowed through her like an electrical current. She took a deep breath, smiled to Ms. Hanson, and went to open the door.

Asher was standing there, and he looked so handsome!

When he left the hotel, leaving Skyler in the very capable hands of a babysitter the hotel recommended, he was jittery. It had been a long time since he'd asked a woman out, preferring to avoid them altogether had been his mantra since the divorce. But now, seeing Hannah dressed up, her hair tied into a loose bun, and smiling at him, Asher wondered if he wasn't being a little crazy. "Hi," He whispered, his smile matching hers.

Stepping towards him, a small wave to Ms. Hanson, Hannah said, "Hi," in return.

They walked across the porch, down the steps, and to where his car was parked.

Asher opened the door for Hannah, his fingers brushing her arm as he waited for her to get in. The prickles of electricity between them ran up his arm, making him smile wider.

Hannah was taking deep breaths as Asher walked around the car to get into the driver's seat. "Whoa," She said aloud, and tried to get her heart into a calmer rhythm.

Once Asher got into the car, he was on high alert. Having Hannah so close to him was like putting a flame next to a keg of gun powder. He didn't know if he would get through the evening without imploding.

Watching Asher, his features only illuminated by the interior lights of the car, Hannah felt completely exposed. They were both fully clothed, but it didn't seem to matter to her insides. In an effort to calm herself internally, Hannah took a few deep breaths and concentrated on her hands that were now knotted together on her lap.

The drive to the restaurant took only a few minutes, and Asher was surprised that they didn't talk. He was nervous, so maybe Hannah was too. The thought made him smile, and he confessed to her, "I was so nervous, coming over to pick you up."

When Asher said the words, Hannah's whole being took a collective sigh, and she settled. She was relieved, and responded, "Thank goodness, I thought it was just me."

Chuckling, Asher pulled the car into the parking lot, just behind the restaurant. He shut off the vehicle and turned to face Hannah. "No," He whispered, "I haven't done this in a really long time, Hannah. I hope you'll be kind and understand that I'm rusty."

How was it that he could be asking her forgiveness when he was the kindest man, besides her father, that she'd ever met? If more men would be as considerate, Hannah doubted that her friends would complain as much as they did about their husbands and boyfriends. "Okay," She told him, "I'll reserve judgement on your dating skills until you've dropped me off."

Smiling at her teasing, Asher started to relax. "Deal," He said, and got out to go around the car and open the door.

They walked around the building to the front of the restaurant, and were greeted by a nice hostess. She showed them to a table, near the front of the restaurant, which provided a beautiful view of the beach.

Hannah sat down, impressed that Asher pulled her chair out for her first, and then sat down.

They each took the menus that the hostess provided, and proceeded to discuss the items listed.

Surprised by Asher's extensive knowledge of seafood, which she herself shared, Hannah smiled when he suggested they get meals and then share them. It was an intimate suggestion, but one she found interesting enough to agree to. After they placed their drink orders, Hannah asked him, "And how is Miss Skyler this evening?"

Smiling at the mention of his daughter, Asher informed Hannah that Skyler told him, "Have a good time and don't worry about me."

She could well imagine the adorable little girl's expression as she told her dad that. Hannah smiled, and asked him, "How did you manage to raise such a doll?"

His eyebrows raised, Asher decided to educate Hannah about the goings on between him and his daughter. "I don't think I raise her, most of the time it seems like she's raising me."

That response made Hannah giggle. "Really?" She asked him.

"Oh yeah," Asher nodded his thanks to the server as she put down their drinks, "she lets me think I'm the boss, but I think we both know better."

Now that didn't surprise Hannah, but she added, "Well, she's not a child who seems unhappy or desperate for attention, so I think you've done a great job."

Her compliment warmed Asher up from the inside. "Thank you," He replied softly.

The feeling of awareness that Hannah experienced in the car earlier came back again. It made her skin tickle and her heart pound as if it wanted to jump right out of her chest with its intensity. She mumbled, "You're welcome," before turning to the server to place her order, thankful for the momentary respite the act allowed her.

Asher watched Hannah closely. He noticed the slight flush in her cheeks when he complimented her or simply told her thank you for her comments. He got the impression that Hannah hadn't had a man's attention for quite some time. Wanting to slow them up, he collected what few wits he had left, and tried to change the subject. "Well," He started, "I think this will give us some time to get to know one another better."

Curious, Hannah leaned closer, and asked, "What did you want to know about me, Asher?"

The words were innocent enough, as they processed through Asher's mind, but her tone......the tone she used made him think of things that had absolutely nothing to do with having dinner and more to do with both of them alone, in bed. 'STOP IT!' He yelled at himself internally. Swallowing hard, he replied, "Uh," and tried to get his brain cells to engage, "what did you go to school for?" He asked.

The change in subject threw Hannah off a bit. She was thinking he would ask something much more personal. Instead she had to go through her muddled mind and pick out memories. "I was a Marine Biology major," She told him, and stared at her sweet tea, preoccupied with stirring the liquid.

"Ah," Asher returned, "so that's how you knew what to do to save that little turtle."

Nodding, Hannah explained, "I was in the program at A&M down in Corpus Christi for two years, but then dad got sick, and I had to come home."

Not knowing what to say, Asher only nodded, and took in the information. To have that put on your shoulders, at that age, was not something most kids would have been able to do. But Hannah didn't seem to hold a grudge or be affected negatively by it, so he took that as reinforcing his first impression of her, which was of a caring person. "How long was he sick?" He asked, genuinely curious.

"Eight years," Hannah answered, and then took a drink of her tea.

Asher sat there, looking shocked. He knew he must seem like an idiot, but he couldn't imagine having to take care of his parents for eight years.

Seeing the astonishment written on his features, Hannah explained, "He wasn't bed ridden for all that time. The problem was that he lost his driving privileges pretty early on due to his inability to react. Mainly I was his chauffer for about the first four years."

Curious, Asher asked her, "And you didn't continue your studies then?"

A lot of people asked Hannah that exact question. Over the years she provided a myriad of answers but there was no cut-and-dried reason. She just hadn't. "I think" She confessed to him, "that I just felt defeated."

He didn't understand what Hannah meant, so he asked her, "Defeated?"

Opening up this emotional can of worms was going to spew out lots of things. Hannah wasn't sure if she was ready to face the expanse of feelings this was bound to bring up, but she wanted to be honest with Asher. "Well, my mom died when I was a sophomore in high school, and I just took care of my dad after that." She looked down into her glass of tea, hoping to be swallowed up by the cool liquid, and went on, "I was always the one who just took care of everything, so when he told me about the ALS, he was so scared. So, I dropped my life to help him live the rest of his."

Sure that the explanation was merely skimming the surface of her feelings, Asher nodded, and reached across the table to cover her hand with his. He looked into her eyes, and told her, "It was a brave thing to do, Hannah."

Looking away for a moment, Hannah responded, "Brave? I'm not sure about that. I think I felt obligated."

"Do you think your dad thought you felt obligated?" Asher asked her.

The server came over with their plates, and that gave Hannah a minute or so to contemplate the question. When they were alone once again, she looked at Asher, his warm eyes intent on hers, and answered, "I hope not."

Asher knew how he felt about Skyler, he would give his life for his daughter, and he would do anything he could to secure her happiness. It sounded, to him, that Hannah's father was the same kind of man, so he would never willingly try to make his daughter feel bad about taking care of him. "I don't think so," He answered, "I think your dad was just thankful at how much you loved him."

Looking across the table, her food still untouched, Hannah prayed that his words described how her father felt. "Let's hope so," She said, and was ready to change the subject.

Chapter 10

The rest of dinner was spent casually talking about Asher's job as an eighth grade History teacher, Skyler, Ms. Hanson, and Hannah's education.

It was if they'd opened up the can of feelings regarding Hannah's father, and wanted to close it again so they both decided to stick to less involved subjects. The talking was good, each of them divulging little things; likes, dislikes, hobbies, and of course, Skyler's preferences.

Hannah enjoyed watching Asher's expression as he discussed his daughter. It was clear that Skyler was the center of his world, as his child should be, but she could also tell that he was appreciative of conversation with another adult. She laughed at his stories of figuring out how little girls wanted to be independent one minute, but then changed their minds when it came to bugs, imaginary spiders, or other kids who were mean to them. He was a very good story teller, using different inflections to make her laugh, or make her look shocked.

They didn't order dessert, instead Asher asked Hannah, "Would you like to walk along the beach?"

The sun was just starting to set when they left the restaurant. They walked to the nearest crosswalk, and waited for the light to allow them to cross the busy street.

Hannah slipped off her sandals, and linked them over her fingers, while Asher pulled off his socks and shoes, and tied the laces together so he could wear them over his shoulder. The sand still held the warmth from the sun, but was cooler than it was the last few times they'd gone in the hot afternoons.

"How long are you and Skyler staying here?" Hannah asked him after they'd walked for a while.

Looking straight ahead, Asher answered, "The rest of the week," he didn't want to look over at Hannah because he was sure he'd kiss her if he did. "We live up on the north side of Houston, in the Woodlands."

Knowing where that was, Hannah nodded, then commented, "Nice area."

Asher stopped, and motioned for Hannah to sit, before joining her. They faced the gulf, its waves rushing to the shore, reminding him of the racing of his heart. "It is," He said.

It hadn't been so long that Hannah didn't recognize the buildup of anticipation, she hadn't noticed a man in a long time, but a woman didn't forget the way it felt when one was interested in her. "Are you going to kiss me, Asher?" She asked in a slightly shaky voice.

The question made Asher's hands tremble with need to touch her. He looked over, saw Hannah's face cast half in shadow, and told her, "Yes, if you'll let me."

Hannah nodded, "I'll let you," she whispered, and put her hand down on the sand so it covered his.

As he leaned over to kiss Hannah, Asher could only think that he must've been moving in slow motion because it was taking far too long for his lips to meet hers. But when they did…. wham! The shot of power that rammed into his belly was enough to put anyone down for the count. Her lips were soft and tender, yet they demanded something from him too.

Hannah could feel him holding back. The kiss was gentle, but held a whole lot of promise. Not having had this kind of connection in so long, Hannah was impatient. She moved her hands up to cup his cheeks as she deepened the kiss.

Having Hannah take the first step to deepen their contact made Asher burn up with need. He was planning on moving slowly, after all she had just gone through something painful, and he certainly didn't want to add to that, so he swore he'd move at a snail's pace. Apparently Hannah had other plans, and that made him okay to change his own. He turned his upper body toward her, and put his arms around her so he could move her over.

Before Hannah could figure out what Asher was doing, she was sitting on his lap. His lips never left hers, only continued their erotic exploration of hers. It was like being swung high into the air, so your whole body felt free and afraid at exactly the same time.

They stayed there on the beach for some time, kissing. Neither of them pushed the limits of their attraction, since they were in public, but they definitely made sure all attention and care was placed into their kissing.

When Asher finally pulled away, he laid his forehead against Hannah's, and whispered, "Wow!" in a shaky breath.

A giggle made its way up Hannah's throat. She shook her head, and replied, "I was going to say the same thing."

"Hannah," He was about to explain why they couldn't go any further, when she put her finger gently against his lips.

Sensing he was about to give her some excuse, Hannah wanted to reassure him, and said, "No," she leaned forward and replaced her finger with her lips for a quick kiss, then continued on, "I know that neither of us is ready for more, no matter how much we may want it."

The fact that she knew what he was going to say, made Asher feel good on one hand, and scared on the other. No woman, not even his ex-wife, seemed to know him as well as Hannah seemed to in just a few short days. "I do want more," He said in a husky voice, still raw from her kisses.

"Me too," She admitted to him.

With a low growl, Asher gently lifted her up again and set her back beside him. "On that note, I should probably get you home."

It was in her to pout, but Hannah decided that wouldn't do either of them any good. She was an adult, no matter how much she didn't want to be on certain occasions. He was a father, a good one, and she should respect the fact that he was trying to go slow. But, all that time of specifically NOT thinking about men and NOT thinking about her life, came crashing back into her. Suddenly, she felt free, as if she should grab onto whatever she could if it made her happy. That followed with feeling guilty that she felt free. Did that mean that she was secretly glad that she no longer had to take care of her dad? If so, that meant she was a horrible person!

They were walking down the beach, but Hannah was miles away. Asher knew she was going through some internal struggle given that her face contorted into various forms of need, worry, and anguish. He'd done the same thing himself, many times, after his wife left. Of course, that was nothing like actually losing someone to death, but loss was loss, the heart didn't seem to know the difference. "Are you okay?" He asked her, wanting to make things better.

"I think I may be having an issue with survivor's guilt or something," Hannah blurted out, then wanted to suck the words back in, she was so humiliated.

Asher could see Hannah was struggling to regain her composure, but she was embarrassed. "Maybe," He answered, then offered, "or maybe you are just working through your grief. Isn't that what you came here to do?"

Hannah nodded, "I did," but she was still adrift in confusion, and rushed on to say, "But, I'm so happy when I'm with you, and Skyler, and then when I think of my dad, I'm not as sad as I think I should be." There, it was all out of her, like a volcanic explosion.

Not being able to help himself, Asher chuckled. "Do you feel better?" He asked Hannah.

Nodding, Hannah stopped, and turned to watch the waves. It was dark now, the only lights at this end of the beach were from the houses set back. Tears slipped down her cheeks, "He told my aunt that he was worried about what I would do after he was gone."

Her words made Asher's heart squeeze. He, thank goodness, still had his folks and they were a Godsend with helping him with Skyler. "May I ask what she told him?" He asked Hannah as he stepped beside her. He didn't touch her, but kept himself physically separate so he wouldn't confuse her or himself.

Looking over to Asher, then back to the rhythmic waves that caressed the shore, Hannah replied, "She told him I'd be fine."

Smiling, even with the tears, she said, "He's with my mother now, and that brings me comfort."

There were times in Asher's life when he knew he'd never forget an image, or a conversation, and this was one of those times. He would never forget the sight of a young woman, standing there, the wind blowing her hair behind her, crying, and talking about comfort. He thought that maybe Hannah was much wiser than most people probably gave her credit for. Instead of giving her words, he just stepped closer and took her into his arms. To hell with keeping their distance, to hell with all of it, life was too short to worry about whether she was in too much grief or if he was taking advantage. They needed to just take it all in, and just see where it went.

Hannah held onto Asher as if he were one of the buoys she saw in the gulf. He was the one thing that, at least at this moment, could keep her from drowning emotionally.

After a few minutes, they silently released one another, and started back towards the B&B. Hannah knew he probably pitied her and she most certainly didn't want that. She was her own woman, but for eight years, just kind of put that part of herself aside. It would take some time for her to get reacquainted with herself again.

The lights at the back of the house were bright, and they could see Shelby and Payton sitting on the back patio, talking quietly. Ms. Hanson came out with a pitcher of something, and spotted them, calling out, "Hey you two, come on up!"

With a look to Asher, and his nod, Hannah smiled and walked with him up the small hill and over the yard. "What are the three of you up to tonight?" She asked the women.

Shelby spoke first, "We're trying to get Payton to eat something."

Payton shot Shelby a nasty look, and Hannah had to look away quickly to avoid laughing. "Uh, Asher," She said, "this is Shelby and Payton, and you've met, Ms. Hanson."

"Willa," Ms. Hanson told them, and winked at Asher.

Hannah was amused by the blush that worked its way across Asher's cheeks. "Did she eat anything?" She asked Shelby.

Looking more irritated by the second, Payton commented, "I'm right here and can hear you."

Without missing a beat, Hannah shot back, "Well, I'm right here and I'm worried about you."

So surprised by the retort, Payton just sat there and didn't speak. Shelby bit her lip, while Ms. Hanson went back into the kitchen. Asher just stood there, feeling way out of his depth. "I suppose I should be going," He said to Hannah.

"Okay," She answered, and they walked back down the lawn, to where it sloped down into the beach. "I had a great time tonight, thank you," She told Asher, and kissed him, only this time it was a quick kiss since there were six eyes watching them.

Asher smiled, fully aware that they were being eyeballed by the other women. "You are very welcome," And then he asked, "Can we see you tomorrow?"

Smiling, Hannah responded, "I'd be pretty ticked off if you didn't ask."

He was holding her hand, and didn't want to let it go. "We'll come by some time in the late morning then," He told her, finally releasing her hand, and making his way down onto the beach.

Hannah stood there for a few minutes, and watched him until his figure faded into the darkness. When she returned to the patio, she noticed that only Shelby was still there. "Where are Payton and Ms. Hanson?" She asked Shelby.

"Payton," Shelby sighed, "went up to her room, and Ms. Hanson, or as she asked Asher to call her…..Willa," she wiggled her eyebrows while she said the caretaker's name, "said she had some emails to send."

Sitting down across from Shelby, Hannah asked, "So, how was your evening?"

Contemplating her answer for a few moments, Shelby finally answered, "Very interesting."

Her new friend's tone piqued Hannah's interest. "Do tell," She said with a smile.

"An old friend of mine, her name is Bridgette, called me tonight and asked if I could take over her gym while she's on maternity leave," Shelby told her. Seeing the confused look on Hannah's face, Shelby smiled, and explained, "Bridgette was on the same gymnastics team as I was when we were growing up. I decided to quit the sport after college, preferring to help my husband, Kent, with his gymnastics career." She sighed, and had to gather her strength back up. Just saying Kent's name, even after he'd been gone for months, was still a shock to her system. "Anyway, she's pregnant and has had some complications so she's had to go on maternity leave sooner than expected. The lady she had lined up to cover isn't available yet, so she asked me to step in."

There were questions, all sorts of them racing around Hannah's brain. "Okay, first, I didn't know you were a gymnast," She said, smiling. "Second, do you feel up to it? What kind of gym does Bridgette own? How big is it?" As if her manners finally caught up with her, Hannah put her hand over Shelby's and said, "You don't have to answer any of those questions, and it's really none of my business."

Shelby genuinely liked Hannah. They were pretty close in age, had both suffered a terrible loss, and were making efforts to heal. "No," She answered Hannah, "Those are all very good questions. First, I was a gymnast, and still know my way around the gym since Kent was a coach, second, I'm not sure, and we'll have to come back to that one, and third, it's a recreational gym which means that there's no pressure of competition, most of her students are younger kids, and it's pretty basic stuff."

Nodding, Hannah took in all the information Shelby was giving her. She'd been in softball, mostly because of her dad she supposed, but she did love the sport on her own too. She'd proven to be pretty good, but didn't want to be worried about sports in college so she'd quit. It sounded like Shelby, although she didn't compete, was still comfortable with the surroundings. "Maybe," Hannah suggested, "this is what you need then, to sort of "dip your toes in" as it were. Maybe this is what you need to get some footing for yourself."

Another thing Shelby liked about Hannah, she possessed a wisdom that many people, men or women, didn't have at her age. "I think you might be right," She told her friend.

They sat on the patio for a few minutes longer, listening to the sounds of the water, before finally going up to bed.

With the sun low in the sky, but making its way higher by the minute, Hannah woke up and jumped out of bed. She'd slept well, dreaming of Asher and those wonderful kisses. She was excited for Shelby, and maybe a little envious on some level. After all, Shelby now had something to occupy her time whereas Hannah just had a big, empty house to return to. She'd been thinking about it, when she heard her phone go off, indicating an incoming text. It was from Asher,

Good Morning! Hope you slept well, I dreamed of you. Skyler is up and ready to roll, can we take you out to breakfast?

Smiling, Hannah typed back her response,

I think I can be persuaded. I dreamt of you too, by the way.

She got out of bed and was in the bathroom turning on the shower, when her phone went off again,

Can I ask what your dreams were about?

After checking the water temperature, Hannah smiled as she typed on her phone,

A lady doesn't kiss and tell. Luckily for you, I'm no lady. I dreamt of your kisses on the beach, of your hand, how it wrapped around mine and made me feel safe.

As soon as she hit send, Hannah became nervous. The text was more revealing than she wanted. What if Asher thought she was easy? What if he thought she was creepy? Second guesses filled her chest, then she heard the phone beep as it received another text,

Well, although I think we differ in thought on whether you are a lady, the other things you mentioned were in the forefront of my mind. I will tell you that I haven't had a

relationship since the divorce so Skyler has never seen me be affectionate with another woman, other than relatives that is.

Reading his words, Hannah wondered if Skyler was upset by Asher holding her the very first day they met. If she was, she didn't act like it. But, then again, the little girl was pretty distracted. They should take it slow. She typed to him,

Why don't we refrain from any hand holding or kissing in front of her, until we're sure she is okay with it?

Although Asher was relieved that Hannah didn't mind him being worried about their actions in front of Skyler, a part of him was seriously bummed that he wouldn't be able to kiss her or hold her hand. Shaking himself mentally, he reminded himself that it wasn't about him, it was about Skyler. Of course, his body was not on the same page whatsoever.

Chapter 11

Within the hour, Hannah was ready and waiting on the front porch for Asher and Skyler. She smiled brightly as they pulled up to the house. Asher got out, gave her a bright smile. It was so difficult to keep from kissing him, but she managed a smile in return and allowed him to open her car door for her. She settled in, and turned to greet Skyler, "Good morning, Skyler."

"Good morning," Skyler returned. When Asher was back in the driver's seat, Skyler asked, "Daddy, why didn't you kiss Hannah when you saw her? Isn't that what boyfriends are supposed to do?"

The innocence of the questions, and the fact that they were just discussing what Skyler would be okay with, had Hannah and Asher looking at each other, and then breaking out laughing.

Skyler had no idea why they were laughing, but she joined in.

They drove to a small café just a few minutes from the B&B. Hannah probably could've gone anywhere and been okay with it, since she was with Asher and Skyler. "So, Skyler, how was your evening with the babysitter?" She asked as they started to walk toward the door of the café.

Twenty minutes later, Skyler was still telling Hannah about her great time with her babysitter, named Sarah. It was difficult for Hannah to keep up with the little girl, she was talking so fast. Asher had to order for her, since she was too focused on explaining how Sarah braided her hair for her and painted her nails.

Asher could see Hannah wasn't used to Skyler's unstoppable storytelling, so he finally spoke up, "Skyler, why don't we let Hannah have some quiet time to drink her tea."

"Okay, Daddy," Skyler answered, as if she was used to her dad asking for some quiet time. She looked down at the paper placemat and began drawing with some crayons the hostess provided.

Looking up at Hannah, Asher mouthed, 'I'm sorry.'

Hannah was puzzled, and mouthed, 'Why? She's fine.'

Shaking his head, Asher was sure Hannah was just being nice. He knew firsthand how Skyler could go off on a chatty tangent for at least an hour. He loved his daughter dearly, but that was a lot for an adult to endure, especially if they weren't used to it.

Trying to hold back her laughter; Hannah just looked at him. He was different this morning. He wasn't just a guy, and he wasn't just Skyler's dad, he was the man who made her heart swell and her lips tingle from remembered kisses.

They ate, and chatted about going to the beach. Skyler had a mouth full of pancakes when she asked Hannah, "When do you go home Hannah?"

Asher quickly told her, "Please don't talk with food in your mouth Skyler," and looked over at Hannah, waiting for her answer.

"I go home in a few more days," She told Skyler, "but I sure am glad that I met you, your dad, Ms. Hanson, Shelby, and Payton while I was here."

Being a child, Skyler was curious and asked, "Do you miss your daddy any less now?"

The look that Asher shot Hannah was filled with shock. Hannah, understanding that Skyler certainly meant no disrespect in asking, smiled, and leaned toward the little girl, before answering, "You know, I don't think I'll ever miss him less, Skyler, but meeting all of you has helped me understand that even though he's not here with me, he'll always be in my heart."

Considering the words Hannah told her, Skyler looked intense for a few moments, then replied, "I guess that's how it is with my mom."

Now, both Asher and Hannah didn't know what to say. Hoping that Asher wouldn't be upset with her, she asked Skyler, "But you know that your mom is here, she just doesn't live with you?"

Nodding, Skyler looked serious when she answered, "Yeah, but she never calls or visits, so it's like she's in Heaven."

Hannah's heart broke for the little girl. Again, she wondered how any mother could choose her career over her child, but, then again, Hannah herself wasn't a mother so she really had no right to judge someone else. "I'm sorry," She told the little girl, and reached across to hold Skyler's hand.

Watching his daughter, as she told Hannah how she felt, Asher wanted to cry. He didn't cry normally, hated feeling like it, but his daughter was apparently in more pain regarding her mom than he knew. He'd have to sit down with his parents when he got home and discuss what he should do.

The only word Hannah could use to describe the look on Asher's face was agony. His little girl was hurting, and more than she let on, apparently. Not wanting their day to be so heavy, emotionally speaking, Hannah smiled, and told Skyler, "You know what, let's try to have some fun today, and maybe we'll forget what makes us sad."

Skyler nodded eagerly, and smiled at Hannah. "Okay," She answered.

Asher got up to pay for their meal while Hannah took Skyler into the bathroom to "freshen up." Skyler liked the phrase Hannah used, and told him that she was a lady now.

When he met up with them, as they left the restaurant, he whispered to Hannah, "I'm sorry about that."

Surprised, Hannah looked at him, "Don't be," she said, "if she feels like she can talk to me, at least she's talking. That's a good thing."

He was going to help Skyler into the car, when she told him, "I've got it, Daddy. I can do it myself." Now he felt really sad.

Hannah watched Asher get in the car, and wanted to comfort him, he looked so dejected. She put her hand on his arm, and asked him, "Are you okay?"

Sighing, Asher nodded, but knew that Hannah didn't believe him. Probably because it wasn't true.

He pulled out of the diner's parking lot and headed north down the main thoroughfare to find a place for them to park. A few minutes later, he parked the car, and was helping get Skyler's mounds of beach supplies out of the trunk.

The threesome went down to the beach, and scoped out a good spot. Since it was relatively early in the day, the beach wasn't crowded yet.

Skyler was busy setting out her toys, so that gave Hannah and Asher some time to themselves. "It's tough isn't it?" She asked him, after they'd set up their beach chairs and sat down.

"What?" Asher asked, the sadness clear in his tone.

Reaching over, Hannah clasped his hand with hers, before saying, "Hearing something that makes you feel as if she isn't as happy as you thought she was."

Looking over at Hannah, he questioned her with, "How did you know that's what I was thinking?"

Staring into his eyes, and wanting to get lost in them, Hannah managed to answer, "I could see the hurt in your expression when she talked about her mom, and the shock on your face."

He felt worse now since he'd probably ruined the day for Hannah too. "I'm sorry," He mumbled.

"For what?" Hannah asked him, "for hoping that you're doing the best you can for your child? Or for thinking that because she's well-adjusted and friendly that she shouldn't have that little bit of unhappiness where her mother is concerned? I don't think you have anything to be sorry for Asher, you are a great dad." She leaned over and gave him a kiss. It was a short one, but the impact on Hannah's heart made her smile.

They enjoyed the rest of the day, playing at the beach, watching Skyler, and just talking. There was no further mention of her father, or Skyler's mother. Hannah sensed that Skyler's words at breakfast were going to weigh heavily on Asher's mind for some time, and she didn't want to contribute to that.

She was sitting in the chair, enjoying the breeze off the water, when a shadow came over her. Opening her eyes, Hannah was surprised to see Chris, her dad's hospice nurse, standing over her. He wore a very strange look on his face. Since Asher had taken Skyler over to an ice cream truck parked down the beach, she was alone. "Chris," She said, her hand covering her eyes.

"I didn't recognize you at first," Chris said. He'd been enjoying the day with friends, in between assignments, and noticed a woman that looked strangely like Hannah. When he walked over, he realized it was her. "What are you doing here?" He asked Hannah.

There was something in Chris' tone that set Hannah on edge. "I received an invitation to come to Galveston and am here with friends," She answered. Something inside of her warned her to keep the information light.

He nodded, and turned when someone called his name. "We're going out to get some early dinner and hit some clubs, do you want to come along?" He asked.

Hearing the hopefulness in Chris' voice made Hannah realize what the problem was. Chris wanted something more from her than she was willing to give. "Thank you," She told him, and smiled, "but I've already got plans."

Chris nodded, and smiled, but it didn't quite reach his eyes. "I'll see you soon," He told her, before running off to catch up with his friends.

A few minutes later, Asher and Skyler returned, with ice cream melting down their hands. They couldn't eat the treat fast enough to compete with the high, June temperatures. She must have been looking worried or something, because Asher asked her, "What's wrong?" his voice laced with concern.

Hannah waited for Skyler to go back to where her toys were, a few yards away, before answering, "I ran into the guy who was my dad's hospice nurse."

Asher nodded in understanding, then asked, "Is everything okay?"

"Well," Hannah tried to explain, "There is something in the way he speaks to me now, since Dad passed away, that makes me nervous."

Having seen some unhealthy attention paid to people, during his job, and outside, Asher understood her meaning. "Are you scared?" He asked her. "This is nothing to take lightly. Always go with your gut," He told her.

The way he was talking made Hannah feel safe. "I will," She told him, then leaned over and gave him a quick kiss, "thank you."

If getting a kiss from Hannah was a thank you then Asher would need to focus more on making sure she needed to thank him. "You're welcome," He replied, and settled back into his chair.

A few hours later, Skyler was becoming whiny. Asher told her to, "Please go pick up your toys and we'll go back to the hotel for a nap."

That comment had Hannah thinking of her and Asher "napping" and that wasn't the wisest thing. Her whole body shivered with the prospect. Of course, that wasn't a possibility since he was here with his daughter, and Hannah would just need to put those crazy thoughts away for the time being. She was almost embarrassed that she was thinking in such primal terms, but her body was committing mutiny against her mind. "I'll just walk back to the B&B," She told him while he started packing up the towels and chairs.

Asher was confused. He assumed Hannah would go back to the hotel with them. "Okay," He told her, then asked, "Will we see you later?"

"Can I call you?" Hannah asked him. She needed a little time to figure out this whole physical thing she had for the man. It would've been easier had he not looked as sad as he did after breakfast. "I'm just going to check in on Shelby, Payton, and Ms. Hanson and see if they need anything." She hoped the words made him feel less rejected.

Understanding that he couldn't monopolize all of Hannah's time, Asher nodded. He watched as Hannah went over to where Skyler was picking up her toys, and gave his daughter a hug and kiss. He wished it was him that Hannah was hugging and kissing. After Hannah gave him one last wave, she started going down the beach. Asher watched for a long time, until he heard Skyler ask, "Are we going, Daddy?"

When Hannah got back to the B&B, she was surprised to find it empty. Ms. Hanson left a note on a chalkboard in the kitchen saying, 'Went shopping, be back a little later.' As she went upstairs, Hannah couldn't hear anything from either Payton or Shelby's rooms so she went down the hall to her own.

She took a quick shower, to wash off the sand and salt from the Gulf air, and to help her feel better. After slipping on a sun dress from the closet, Hannah went out onto the patio. She sat there, on the chair, and watched the water dance under the sun's rays. There was something very hypnotic about the water, and its interaction with the breezes, sunlight, and even moonlight. She'd been there for a while, when she heard a noise. Turning to face the balcony off of Payton's room, she saw the woman come out with the same blanket she'd seen her hold every day in her hands.

Hannah assumed the blanket was Payton's daughter's and ached for the other woman's turmoil. Her own mother told her that it was okay that she was going before Hannah. "It's how it should be," Hannah remembered her mother telling her. At the time, Hannah simply was too young to understand it.

"Is there anything I can do for you?" Hannah asked Payton.

Surprised by the question, Payton looked up, and stared at Hannah for a few minutes, before answering, "Yes, would you mind joining me?"

The answer completely surprised Hannah. Payton didn't speak much, and to open up like she was now, was a good sign, in Hannah's mind anyway. "Okay," She told her, "I'll be right there."

Walking through her room, she didn't close her door, and also left the door to Payton's room open after she entered. That way Shelby would feel free to join them, hopefully. She noticed that Payton's room was done in varying shades of purple. Mostly shades of lilac. It was very feminine and comfortable. As Hannah walked out onto the patio, she went up to Payton and gave her a hug. It was done out of need, on both their parts.

Payton hugged her back, which surprised Hannah almost as much as the invitation to come over had. She noted that Payton was far too thin, and made a mental note to speak to Ms. Mason about that. "How are you?" She asked Payton.

Gripping the blanket as if it were a lifeline, Payton smiled, but the tears streaking down her cheeks contradicted the motion.

"I've definitely been better," She said, then added, "But I've also been worse."

The ability to recognize yourself and your feelings was a good thing. Hannah read up on grief when her mother passed away, although she didn't let on to her dad that she had. She didn't want to interfere with his grieving process. Then, when he passed away, it was as if all bets were off since she was now alone. "That's a good sign," She told Payton.

As if she'd had an epiphany, Payton smiled, genuinely, and announced, "It is, isn't it?"

Chapter 12

Hannah and Payton sat on the patio and talked for a while. Shelby came upstairs a while later, and they motioned for her to join them.

The three of them discussed their day. Payton was still a lot quieter than Shelby or Hannah, but she was making the effort. A fact that wasn't lost on any of them.

Ms. Hanson came up to find them, and asked if they would all come downstairs for dinner.

As the four women sat down at the table, there was a feeling of connection that was stronger than before. Ms. Hanson asked everyone questions, they were simple ones, just to draw out the women. She asked Hannah, "So, how is that handsome father and his adorable daughter?"

Still feeling a bit conflicted, Hannah answered the question with a short, "They're fine." She watched Ms. Hanson's reaction and knew that the woman would most certainly not let the subject drop that easily.

"If you'd like to invite them over for dinner tomorrow night, you can," Willa informed Hannah.

Hannah's gaze shot over to where Payton sat, staring straight ahead. Even if Ms. Hanson thought it was a good idea, Hannah's gut told her that it was too soon for Payton to be around other children. "I'll pass on the invitation," She answered Ms. Hanson.

Willa looked around the table, and zeroed in on Payton, before saying, "I don't want to cause any of you pain, but it's easier to face the inevitable here, in a somewhat private way,

Danette Fogarty

before you're forced to do it out there," she pointed toward the window. "The pain will be horrible for a long time."

Throwing down her napkin, Payton's temper began to rise. She shouted, "How would you know about my pain?" to Ms. Hanson.

"It's been fifteen years, two months, and 4 days since I lost my son," Willa said quietly.

The comment sat there, drifting in the air between the women. Since Hannah already knew about Ms. Hanson's loss, she didn't say anything. Shelby gasped though and stared at Payton. It was as if the air had been let out of a balloon, Payton collapsed back into her chair and stared at Ms. Hanson.

Willa took a moment to compose herself, and explained, "My husband, Jack, and I were sitting down to dinner. I remember because it was lasagna, Jack's favorite. We were just starting to eat when there was a knock on the door." She dabbed her mouth with her napkin to remove non-existent food. "I figured it was James, coming over to beg for dinner," She smiled at the memory, "he did that a couple times a week." Willa looked at Payton directly. "There was a police officer at the door, he was holding his hat in his hand, and it didn't occur to me, at first that there was bad news." Willa fought back the tears that wanted to fall. "Anyway, he asked if I was Mrs. Hanson, and I nodded," She cleared her throat before continuing, "Jack had joined me by then, I'm not sure why he did, but having him there was better." She recalled the memory in vivid detail. "And the officer told us that James was killed." Willa looked around the table, making eye contact with all three women, before saying, "You see, he'd driven by a bar, and there was a man who was hitting a woman outside the building. Jack stopped to intervene." She smiled, "His father and I always taught him to help others, especially women. But the man who was abusing her had a knife, and stabbed James multiple times."

The gravity of the story hit them all solidly in the chest. Hannah couldn't speak for the others, but she'd been blindsided by information. What a horrible way to lose a loved one, all because they were trying to help someone else.

Willa watched them, as the information sank in, and hurt for them. It was necessary, sometimes, to share your own pain so that others could understand that you truly knew what they were experiencing. "The woman whom Jack saved has since become a family advocate attorney, and every year, she sends me flowers."

Silence filled the room.

Hannah watched the other women, wondering what they were thinking. Her eyes widened as Payton finally stood up, walked over to Ms. Hanson, and fell to her knees in front of the woman, hugging her. Looking at Shelby, who was beginning to cry herself, Hannah allowed the tears to come. She and Shelby watched as Ms. Hanson comforted Payton, and held her as if she were a child.

With a quiet understanding between them, Hannah, followed by Shelby, got up to clear the dinner dishes. Payton, still in Ms. Hanson's arms, was talking quietly so they couldn't hear her. It wasn't their business anyway, so they just took the dishes into the kitchen, put away the leftovers, and filled the dishwasher with the used dishes. They were just finishing up when Ms. Hanson came into the room.

"Thank you, girls," Willa said, a smile on her face. "You certainly didn't have to do that."

Shelby smiled, and returned, "I'm sorry about your son, but I'm sure that your loss helped Payton feel as though someone understands what she's going through."

Willa smiled, "She's very angry, and I have to admit that I went through that too."

Hannah walked over and gave Ms. Hanson a hug, before saying, "Maybe you need to talk to Shelby too."

Looking confused, Shelby asked, "About what?"

"Not tonight, dear," Willa told the women, "we'll save that for another day." She was tired, and the look on her face showed it. "I'll just retire for the night, and I'll see you at breakfast," She told them before going through the door that led to her suite of rooms.

Picking up a serving tray, and putting it away in the cupboard, Hannah was surprised to see Shelby looking at her expectantly when she turned back around. "Oh, did you need something?" She asked Shelby.

Perhaps Hannah could fool others, but Shelby could spot a cover up a mile away. "You are very good at taking care of others," She told Hannah, "but don't forget that you are supposed to take care of yourself too."

Hannah stood in the kitchen for a long while after Shelby left. She wondered what her new friend meant by the comment.

When Hannah went upstairs to her room, she remembered that she'd told Asher she'd give him a call. It wasn't very late so she picked up her phone and dialed his number. She smiled when he answered on the first ring, saying, "Hello, there."

"Hello, yourself," Hannah said quietly.

There was something in her tone that sounded serious, and Asher picked up on it right away. He asked her, "Are you okay?"

Before thinking too much about it, Hannah blurted out, "I'm not okay. I'm mad that my dad died, and I'm sad for my new friends, and I'm happy that I met you and Skyler, and all of that makes me feel really confused."

Asher could only guess at what it must be like, having those around you feeling the grief you yourself were feeling. He'd gone through similar feelings when his marriage ended, but Hannah made him realize that they were not even on the same level as what she and the other ladies at the B&B were experiencing. "Do you want to come over?" He asked her. "Skyler just went down for the night, thank goodness, and I'm just sitting here, contemplating whether or not to open a bottle of wine."

The invitation, although a surprise, sounded wonderful. "If you think it's okay?" She returned.

"I wouldn't have asked you, Hannah, if I didn't want to see you." He whispered. The emotion laced with the words made his heart skip into a triple rhythm.

Hannah smiled, "Okay, then. Give me the address, and I'll be there as soon as I can." She answered.

It took Hannah about twenty minutes to "freshen up" after she hung up with Asher. She didn't want to go over to his hotel room smelling of the beach and having sand on her, so she showered quickly and then put her hair up. She pulled out a brightly floral sundress, her sandals, and quietly left her room.

She was halfway down the hall when she heard a door open. Shelby poked her head out, and asked, "Are you going on a late night rendezvous?" She asked a guilty looking Hannah.

"Uh, it's only 8:45pm so it's not that late, but I am going over to see Asher," Hannah whispered her reply.

With a nod, Shelby whispered back, "Have fun, and I'll cover for you if you're not back by breakfast."

Not even considering that she'd stay over at Asher's hotel room, Hannah's eyes widened, "I'm not staying over," she told Shelby, a blush covering her cheeks.

Smiling, and shaking her head slowly, Shelby replied, "Like I said, I'll cover for you if you're not back." She turned to go back into her room, and threw a "Goodnight," over her shoulder as she did.

Hannah couldn't help but smile. She was kind of sneaking out, and going over to a man's hotel room. The two things did sort of lend to assumptions. She hadn't brushed her hair until it shone in the light, and she hadn't made sure to use her best perfume just to go for a visit. Then again, Skyler was there, having a six-year-old didn't necessarily make for a sexy sleepover arrangement.

Shaking off her thoughts, Hannah continued downstairs and out the front door.

The drive to Asher's hotel room took just a few minutes. He was staying at one of the huge hotels along the beachfront. She parked on the street, making sure to use her parking meter app so she didn't have to worry about getting towed, and proceeded to walk into the lobby.

It was an upscale place, the staff acknowledged her presence, and she went to the bank of elevators across from the front desk.

After getting in, she pushed the button for his floor, and started to feel unsure about this. Was this a "booty call" her friends used to brag about in college? If her thoughts about her and Asher, earlier on the beach, were any indication, it could definitely lead in that direction. When the elevator dinged, as it reached the floor Asher's room was on, Hannah actually jumped a little from the nerves pulsing through her.

She walked down the long corridor, and located the room number he'd given her. It was only a little before nine in the evening, so there were still a good number of people milling about. Some were going out, and some just coming in. Taking a deep breath to calm her emotions, Hannah softly knocked on the door.

Asher had been sitting on pins and needles since Hannah told him she was coming over. Oh, he wanted to see her. When they parted ways this afternoon, he couldn't deny the disappointment at the fact that she wasn't coming back here with them. The funny thing was, he'd never even given a thought to that before meeting Hannah. There'd been plenty of women who "made it clear that they were available" to him after the divorce. With the emotional anguish his ex-wife left in her wake, he just wasn't interested.........until Hannah.

There was a knock on the door, and he was pulled out of his thoughts. Going over, he peeked through the peep hole to see her standing there, looking nervous. He could definitely relate to that thought. Opening up the door, he smiled, and told Hannah, "Come in."

Hannah went into the hotel room, her hands clasped together so tightly that her knuckles were white. "I, uh," She stammered, "I didn't bring any wine or anything with me, sorry."

'Yep,' Asher thought to himself, 'she's just as nervous as you are.' "You didn't need to bring anything," He leaned over and kissed her lightly, "except yourself."

Her insides were now turning to that gooey stuff that was inside a candy bar, but Hannah couldn't think of what it was called since her brain disengaged with the kiss Asher gave her.

Taking Hannah's hand, Asher led her through the small living room and out onto a small balcony. There was a table there, and the view of the Gulf was breathtaking. The lights from all the hotels along the strip of highway cast enough elimination that you could see the water hitting the beach clearly. "This is lovely," She said, and sat down in the chair he pulled out for her.

After sitting down across from her, Asher asked, "Can I get you anything? Water? Soda? Wine?"

Shaking her head no, Hannah turned so she was facing him. "I was so nervous coming over here, Asher, I don't know what this means."

Asher couldn't deny that her innocence made his insides churn with need. Although, she could say just about anything, and his insides would go on full alert. "Hannah," He reached over and covered her hands with his, "It means whatever you want it to." Knowing he should be clear, he explained, "I don't have women over when Skyler's here, to stay over, I mean." He smiled, "Actually, I've not had a woman over since the divorce."

She still had questions, "So you don't want me to stay over?" She asked him.

The question she asked was complicated on about ten different levels. "Oh, I want you to stay over," He said eagerly, "but I don't want to confuse Skyler, and I don't want either of us to get muddled up into the physical aspect of a relationship until you're sure."

Things were becoming clearer for Hannah, "Asher, I think I'm ready for a physical relationship with you," she smiled and squeezed his hand, "I think about you, and those kisses, all the time."

Her words made his body sizzle, and she didn't even realize the power she had over him in that area. "I'm not going to pretend that I don't want that either, but let's just say that we'll take it off the table, so to speak, for tonight."

"Deal," She said, then proceeded to get up and walk around the table to where he sat. His eyes held questions, so she told him, "But that doesn't mean we can't have some more of those kisses." She held out her hand, and tugged it as he stood up. She walked into the living room, sat down on the couch, and pulled him down beside her. "I think this would be more comfortable," She told him.

If only she knew what she did to him? Asher wondered how he'd gotten away with not feeling anything for this long. She put him under some crazy spell of hopes and wants and dreams that he'd almost forgotten even existed. "I think so too," He answered her before sitting down beside her and wrapping her up into his arms.

Their kisses, although somewhat hesitant at first, built up quickly into long streams of touches, and whispers combined with quiet moans of pleasure. He pulled her onto his lap, and lavished her mouth with all of his attention. It was if they fed off of one another's needs. Hannah was a giving kisser, following his lead sometimes, and taking the initiative others. There were a few times when they were each gasping for breath, so they had to break the connection between their lips. She would lay her head on his shoulder, and kiss his neck. Sweet, tentative kisses, that drove him crazy. He would turn and capture her lips once again and start all over.

Hannah's insides heated up so much when Asher kissed her that she thought she might just burst into flames and vanish into ashes. And she couldn't sit still, the urge to move against his, pretty apparent, arousal, made her feel powerful. She would move her bottom just a bit, and the moan it elicited from him made her smile. Her hands were on his shoulders, neck, cheeks, and arms. It was as if they were completely independent and sought their own satisfaction.

Finally, hours later, which really only felt like minutes, they slowed their kisses. Hannah rested her head on his shoulder, and she must've drifted off because the next thing she knew, she was alone on the sofa, a small blanket covering her, and the sun was shining through the glass doors.

Sitting up, she glanced at the clock and was shocked at the time. There were two doors off of the living room, and she assumed one was Skyler's and one was Asher's. Since she had no idea who's was whose, she got up, grabbed her purse, along with her phone, and headed out the door.

She was pulling into the spot she'd vacated the night before at the B&B only minutes later. As quietly as she could, she went inside and started upstairs, only to see a smiling Ms. Hanson standing at the doorway to the dining room. "Is this a walk of shame?" She asked Hannah, teasingly.

"Well," Hannah looked at Ms. Hanson with a smirk, "I am getting in at," she glanced at her phone, "about 6:30am, but I didn't sleep with anyone." She felt like she was busted after being out past curfew.

Willa nodded, "Nope, no walk of shame then," she smiled, and asked Hannah, "Did you have a good time?"

Sighing, Hannah answered, "I most definitely did."

Waving for Hannah to proceed up the stairs, Willa turned back toward the kitchen, and giggled to herself. She remembered those days with great fondness.

Chapter 13

Hannah plopped down on her bed, still clothed, and proceeded to fall asleep.

She woke up, hours later, a smile pasted on her face. She may not have had a "walk of shame" but she was sure happy about the hours of kissing she shared with Asher the night before. He'd been so considerate, alleviating her fears of what his physical expectations might be. A gentleman, she thought, and then wondered how much of a gentleman he would be in bed.

That erotic train of thought needed to be derailed ASAP! Getting up, Hannah jumped into the shower. Although the cool water helped calm her heightened nerves, the thoughts of Asher continued to fill her mind with remembered kisses and touches.

When she came downstairs, Shelby, Payton, and Ms. Hanson were sitting at the dining room table. She knew that Ms. Hanson had revealed her arrival time since they were all looking at her smugly. "Good morning," She said brightly, trying to ignore the looks.

"Try good afternoon," Shelby supplied.

Looking at her phone, Hannah groaned inwardly. It was, in fact, afternoon. That would explain the sandwiches and fruit that were currently set out on the table. "I, er, you're right, sorry."

Payton actually giggled, which caused everyone else to look at her. "What?" She asked when she noticed their looks, "It's funny to get caught slinking in during the early morning hours."

Thinking about it, Hannah started to laugh, "It is, isn't it?" She asked rhetorically.

They ate lunch, and stayed at the table chatting for some time afterward. It was Hannah's and Shelby's last day at the house. Payton was leaving the day after they were, and everyone now seemed reluctant to go.

Ms. Hanson darted in and out of the room, refilling glasses of tea and lemonade. She'd sit down for a few minutes, but then a timer would go off in the kitchen and she'd scurry out. If the smells filling the house were any indication, then she was making something tasty for dessert, after dinner.

They were still talking when Hannah heard her phone go off, indicating a message. She saw it was from Asher,

I've waited as long as I could before texting you. I told Skyler that you'd come over to "visit" last night and she's been pouting since. We both miss you.

His words made her stomach tumble around as if she'd stuck it in the dryer. She texted back,

I miss you both too, what are your plans today?

Shelby winked at Payton, before saying, "With a smile like that, it must be the new boyfriend who's texting."

Rolling her eyes, Hannah nodded. "Yes, it's Asher, if you must know."

Payton spoke up, "I remember those days with my ex, the not being able to stand being apart."

Both Hannah and Shelby stared at Payton. Her words were spoken with emotion, the good kind, and although they were shocked, they were both glad that she was coming out of her shell.

Hannah's phone went off again, she read what Asher wrote,

We're going to go over to Moody Gardens for some exploration and then get in some beach time. Interested in joining us? Bring a change of clothes for dinner, Skyler thinks we should take you out.

Hannah didn't care who came up with the idea, she loved it. She typed back,

I'm visiting with Shelby and Payton but can meet you on the beach in a couple of hours, if that's okay?

Shelby exaggerated a sigh, "Geez," she said to Hannah, "just go!"

Smiling at Shelby and Payton, Hannah stuck out her tongue. "I'm meeting him in a little while, okay?" She teased her friends.

Sitting forward, Payton asked the other two women, "Can we please make a pact to keep in touch? I can sure use the back up."

Hannah nodded, and Shelby told Payton, "Of course! We're friends now, you can't shake us."

The three of them laughed.

Just as she'd texted, Hannah was walking up to where Asher and Skyler were playing in the sand, a couple of hours later. After her talk with the girls, she'd run upstairs and shoved a sun dress, brush, lip gloss, and a towel into her beach bag and all but ran down the sandy stretch of beach to find them. They were sitting in the sand, building a sand castle when Hannah found them. "I don't think it's big enough," She said, smiling.

Skyler jumped up first, and ran over to where Hannah stood. "Daddy said you came to our hotel room last night, why didn't you wake me up?" She demanded.

Crouching down, Hannah held Skyler's hands in her own, "I just wanted you to get some rest so we could be on the beach today."

The way Skyler was looking at her, Hannah wasn't sure if the little girl was buying the reasoning or not. But, after a few seconds, Skyler nodded, and went back to building her sand castle. Then it was Asher's turn. He got up and walked over to Hannah. This time, he did kiss her. It wasn't as intense as the passionate kisses they'd share the night before, but it still packed a wallop to Hannah's body. "Thank you," She whispered to him.

"For what?" He asked Hannah, wanting to kiss her more, but knowing now wasn't the time.

Smiling up at him, the sun making his hair look lighter, he looked like he belonged here, on the beach. "For making me smile," Hannah answered.

He gave her a strange look, and nodded, before going back over to where Skyler had resumed building her sand castle.

Hannah watched the two of them for a while. She'd spread out her beach towel and used her beach bag to hold down one end of it. Watching Asher and Skyler work together, laughing here and there at some antic one of them did, was relaxing.

Asher could feel Hannah's eyes on him, and he felt exposed. When she said thank you for making her smile, he was suddenly overwhelmed with emotion. It was if his heart decided it no longer wanted to be inside his chest so it leapt. The feeling made him feel a little out of control. He couldn't say anything in return.

She was leaving tomorrow, and Asher wondered what he would do then.

After Skyler announced that the sand castle was finished, Hannah clapped. It was difficult not to notice Asher's distance from her. She'd upset him somehow, she sensed it, but she wouldn't lie to him about how she felt when she was with him.

The three of them took their beach paraphernalia to the car and tucked it in the trunk, before going off to search for food.

Hannah and Asher were each on one side of Skyler, and Asher was relieved that his daughter was a bit of a buffer.

They ended up picking a local deli to eat at, and grabbed a booth by the window. The place was filled with beachgoers looking for a quick bite at the end of their day.

Since Skyler was, once again, enthralled with her coloring, Hannah asked Asher, "Is everything okay?"

He wanted to say yes, and he almost nodded, but it would have been a lie. Instead, he told her, "No."

That one little word had Hannah's system going on full alert. Her appetite left immediately and she ordered only a small salad for her dinner. "Can you explain?" She asked him softly.

Asher felt like a first-class jerk. Clearly, he'd upset Hannah with his behavior today. He just couldn't put his feelings into a specific category, and the feeling of unsteadiness knocked him off kilter. "You're leaving tomorrow, right?" He asked Hannah.

She nodded, then answered, "Yes."

Sitting there, in a crowded deli, his daughter right beside him, and Hannah across from him, he felt totally alone. "I'm upset," He murmured.

Did he think she wasn't upset about leaving? His kisses said one thing, but his behavior and clipped tone this afternoon said something else. She leaned over, her brow creased with emotion, "And you think I'm not?" she asked him.

Asher's eyes met Hannah's, across the table, and it was tangible, this feeling of connection between them. It made him want to laugh and cry at the same time. Her face reflected his feelings, he could see she was torn up too. So why was he acting like this? 'Because you feel like she's leaving you.' He answered internally. Reaching across the table, he wrapped his fingers around hers, loving the way her skin felt beneath his fingertips. "No," He whispered, hoping Skyler didn't hear too much, "I'm being selfish."

His words sunk in and Hannah smiled. He was telling her that he didn't want her to go. Asher seemed to be a pretty open person, so it shouldn't have surprised Hannah that, feeling how he appeared to feel, he would be a little upset that they were now separating. "You're not," She told him, and went on to say, "You're feeling what I'm feeling, something new and wonderful and you don't want to let real life get in the middle of it all just yet."

How did she know exactly how he felt? This ability of hers to peg him so perfectly, was more than a little unnerving. Nodding at Hannah, he rubbed his thumb across the back of her hand. Her skin was so soft, and he wanted to feel every inch of her.

Hannah watched the change in Asher's features, and blushed. It wasn't difficult to see where his thoughts ran off to, when his eyes darkened into a deep brown, almost black color.

Her pulse picked up in response, and she lifted their joined hands to kiss the tips of his fingers.

What should have been a simple kiss, on his hand no less, sent a tidal wave of need through Asher's system. Oh, she had him! Knowing it both scared the hell out of him, and made him happy at the same time.

Their food came and Skyler dug in, as if she hadn't eaten in ages. She would ask her father or Hannah a question periodically, but seemed quite content to eat her dinner and color on the paper placemat.

After they ate, they walked back to the car, and drove to the hotel where Asher and Skyler were staying. Skyler was the only one keeping up any conversation, asking the adults about the water, the beach, a bicyclist she'd seen, and chatting non-stop.

Hannah and Asher answered Skyler's questions, but otherwise they were quiet.

Asher parked in the parking garage and they all three got out to collect what they needed to take inside. Skyler was between them, holding their hands, and singing a song she learned from school.

They were walking through the lobby, when Hannah heard a lady comment, "Look at that adorable little girl, she looks like her mother." Although she was flattered that the woman thought she was Skyler's mother, the comment also poured a cold dose of reality over Hannah's feelings. She had questions she needed to ask Asher; about him, about her, and especially about Skyler.

Opening up the hotel room door, Asher smiled at his daughter. She was spent from the day at the beach. He figured they had enough time to get her in a bath, in pajamas, and maybe a quick snack before she'd pass out for the night. Truthfully, he was somewhat relieved. Looking over at Hannah, he smiled.

'The man's smile could melt an iceberg,' Hannah thought to herself. Holy Cow, she was ready to jump his bones right here, and his daughter was only a few feet away. Fighting her crazy thoughts, she asked Skyler, "So, what's the routine here?"

"Well," Skyler looked at Hannah, a devious smile on her face, "Daddy usually lets me stay up late since we're on vacation."

Asher smiled, and cleared his throat, "You might want to be a little more truthful, young lady."

Knowing she was caught, Skyler looked contrite, "Okay, Daddy," she answered, then looked at Hannah to say, "bath, snack, and then bed."

Trying not to laugh at the range of emotions Skyler displayed all in the last minute and a half, Hannah was smitten. The little girl could have told her anything, and she'd believe it. "Well, why don't we ask your dad if a bubble bath is okay?"

Her eyes lighting up, Skyler looked hopefully at Asher, and asked him, "Can we have a bubble bath, Daddy?"

Not quite sure where they would get bubble bath from, he told them, "Uh, sure, but I didn't bring any bubble bath with me."

Grateful for Ms. Hanson's earlier suggestion, Hannah reached into her bag and pulled out a little gift bag. She handed it to a delighted Skyler, and watched the little girl open it.

"Wow!" Skyler exclaimed. The princess bag was filled with little gifts; a bottle of bubble bath, some nail polish, a princess brush, and a matching princess purse. "Daddy, look!" Skyler showed him the gifts.

Not only did Hannah seem to get him, but she certainly had Skyler pegged too. He watched the happiness his daughter wore, and knew he was in deep trouble with his feelings for Hannah. "That was so nice of Hannah, you should thank her," He said, trying to keep his emotions under control.

Hannah was watching Skyler, and was smiling. "I wanted you to know that I was thinking about you, since I'm leaving tomorrow." The words hung in the air between the three of them, and now Hannah wished she hadn't spoken them out loud.

"Bubble bath," Asher said, breaking the tension.

Skyler jumped up and ran into the bathroom, saying, "C'mon Hannah," over her shoulder.

Not hesitating, Hannah followed her orders, smiling as she went.

Chapter 14

Two hours later, Hannah was standing in the doorway, watching a, now sleeping, Skyler. She helped Skyler with her bubble bath, where they ended up getting as much water outside the tub as was in it. Then Hannah painted Skyler's fingernails and toenails. It was tough, since she was such a little girl, but she loved the attention from Hannah. After that was done, Skyler demanded that Hannah be the one to read her a bedtime story, although Asher was at least allowed to be in the room. Before she read half the book, Skyler was sleeping.

Asher came up behind Hannah, and put his hands on her shoulders. He smiled at the fact that she was watching Skyler sleep, and told her, "I do that too, just watch her sleep."

Smiling herself, Hannah leaned back into him. She loved the solidness of him. "How does it feel to have a little piece of yourself running around?" She asked him.

"Overwhelming, scary, wonderful," Asher answered, and gently pulled her away from the doorway before closing the door behind them. He steered her into the living area of the suite, and continued, "I love her more than I thought I could, and I get angry at the drop of a hat if I feel like she's being picked on."

They walked to the kitchenette, and Hannah sat at the bar as he pulled out a bottle of wine. He held it up, silently asking if she'd like some. She nodded yes, then said, "You're a great dad."

The way Hannah said the words made Asher think that she was probably thinking of her own dad, so he asked her, "Like your dad?"

She couldn't help it, Hannah chuckled, "Yes," she answered. "He was a pretty cool guy, but he was a great dad!"

Asher put the glasses of wine on the bar, and walked around so he was standing in front of her. "I imagine that he passed on some of his finest qualities to his daughter."

The air was changing, very fast. They were not really talking about parenting anymore, it was more about them as a couple. "You were pouting earlier, weren't you?" Hannah asked him.

His hands were on both side of her, his fingers ached to touch her, and he answered, "Yes."

Appreciating his honesty, Hannah ran her hands up his arms, and rested them on his shoulders. "Me too," She whispered, and waited for him to kiss her.

His head dropped, his eyes focused on her lips, and Asher couldn't think of anything he wanted to do more than kiss Hannah. When his lips touched hers, it was like twisting an already taut rubber band, tighter. Her lips were eager, matching his as they tasted, nipped, and explored hers.

Hannah wanted to be enveloped, and that's what Asher's kisses did to her. He tucked her inside this little safe place where there was only the two of them.

Asher stepped closer, and pulled Hannah up against him. His arms were around her now, running absently up and down her back. Her mouth was soft, pulling him into some kind of sensual trance. Out of breath, he lifted his head a few inches, and looked into her eyes. Her gray eyes were dark and tumultuous, like the churned up waves during a storm. "You're beautiful," He whispered, and pulled her back to him.

Oh, the feeling of being swept up into a crazy tornado of sensations made Hannah feel restless. She wanted more, and ran her fingers through Asher's hair. Her kisses intensified, and she sucked lightly on his bottom lip.

Asher was now gasping for breath. She stole it from him, or maybe he just forgot to breathe when he was kissing her. Either way, it turned him inside out. Leaning his forehead against hers, he asked, "Are you going to stay here tonight?"

The question surprised Hannah. She wasn't sure what to say. She wanted to stay, but there were other considerations besides her wants. "What about Skyler?" She asked.

Feeling so stirred up, Asher hadn't thought about anything except being with Hannah. Although he should feel ashamed for not considering his daughter, he didn't. "She's sleeping," He whispered, "and she's in her own room, I sleep in there," he pointed to another door on the other side of the suite.

"What if she wakes up and sees me in your bed?" Hannah asked. She wanted to just throw out all reason, but she couldn't.

Smiling, Asher answered, "That child hasn't woken up during the night since she was an infant, she sleeps like a log, but I'll come up with something if she does," he kissed her, "Hannah, I don't want you to leave here tonight. Stay." He cupped her face between his hands, and whispered, "Stay here with me, and let's make love."

How did a woman say no to that? Hannah couldn't. "Okay," She whispered back. "Let me just text Shelby so someone knows where I am, okay?" She asked him.

Asher nodded, and was filled with relief. He wasn't sure she would stay, hell, he wasn't sure asking her to stay was the right thing to do. She was right, Skyler was in the other room. But he felt this overwhelming desperation when he thought about

Hannah. He wanted to be with her and not let her go. "I'm going to go and shower quickly, you join me when you're done with your text, okay?" He asked her.

Looking up into his intense gaze, Hannah croaked out, "Oh, okay." She waited until he'd gone through the doorway to his room, then walked over to where her phone was, and typed,

It's Hannah. Asher asked me to stay over. I know it may not be right, but I want to. Can you cover for me with Ms. Hanson?

Shelby's phone went off, so she picked it up. A smile formed on her face, and she looked up to see a curious Ms. Hanson and Payton facing her, "Oh, that was Hannah, she's having a sleepover with Asher."

Payton's eyebrows rose, but she remained silent. Ms. Hanson, however, responded, "Well, good for her."

Laughing at their combined reactions, Shelby typed back,

I'm with her and Payton and we all say, have a good time. ☺

Hannah blushed when she read the reply. Oh geez, did everyone need to know she was sleeping with Asher? Putting the phone back into her purse, she picked up her beach bag, and went through the half-opened door Asher went through earlier.

The room was dark, the only light coming from the bathroom on the opposite side of it. Hannah's pulse pounded so loudly, she wondered if her heart would hop out of her chest. She put down her purse and beach bag on top of the dresser and peeled off her sun dress.

She'd never walked naked into a room with a man before. During college there'd been one guy, Gary, who she'd lost her virginity to, but that wasn't like this. This was a whole different universe of awareness. Her body literally tingled, knowing that Asher would be touching it. With more nerve than she actually felt, she walked over to the bathroom door, and slowly pushed it open.

The shower was running, and she could see Asher's head through the top of the shower curtain. Her body filled with anticipation, and she crossed the few feet to the shower. "I'm nervous," She announced.

Asher knew the second that Hannah was in the room with him, he'd felt her, deep down in his bones. He purposely didn't look at her, wanting to make her feel as comfortable as possible. When she told him she was nervous, he looked over. Although the bottom of the shower curtain was opaque, the top was clear. He saw her, standing just a foot away from him, her shoulders rising and falling with the deep breaths she was taking. "Me too," He answered, and reached for the end of the shower curtain to pull it open for her.

If Asher had offered her empty platitudes or tried to "convince" her, she might've chickened out. But he hadn't, he'd admitted that he was nervous too. With another deep breath, she stepped into the shower. Before she could say anything, Asher pulled her too him, and kissed her.

Within seconds, Hannah was consumed in a powerful tide of want that she had no inclination to get out of. She didn't see his body, instead, she felt it beneath her fingertips. It wasn't difficult to discern that he was aroused, she felt his hardness press against her. She skimmed her fingers down his sides, his shoulders, his back, his neck, and leapt into the sensations as if they were a lifeline.

Feeling Hannah pressed up against him, Asher's body tightened. She was exploring him, and he somehow was able to keep his hands on her shoulders. He wanted to allow her to take the lead for now. This was the first time he'd been with a woman since his ex-wife, and he felt like a teenager, full of impulses and no control.

Hannah sunk into her feelings like she was slipping into warm water, she finally moved his hand down from her shoulder until it covered her breast. As soon as his fingertip touched her hardened nipple, she moaned into his mouth.

He was feeding off of Hannah's arousal, Asher knew that. When he heard her moan, he had to taste her. So he lifted his head, smiled down at her, and then got on his knees and lavished her nipple with his mouth, giving it the attention he knew they both wanted.

"Oh, God," Hannah was clutching his head with her hands, her head thrown back. The hot water, combined with Asher's loving made her feel as if she would combust at any moment.

Asher switched to the other breast, nipping and sucking it until he could feel Hannah panting with desire. Moving his hand downward, he felt her thigh and slowly moved his hand in between her legs. His fingers found her center, spreading her swollen lips, and reaching inside.

Hannah gasped as Asher touched her intimately. Any reality of sex she thought she knew was thrown out the proverbial window. Any possible talents she may have thought Gary possessed were long gone. Asher knew how to please a woman, or at least he knew how to please her. "Ahhh," She sighed.

Smiling against her breast, Asher moved his fingers until one was inside her moist heat and one was on her swollen clit. He moved his fingers until Hannah was shaking. Now she was ready.

Hannah went from standing up, to being lifted up into Asher's arms in a matter of seconds. His mouth found hers and made love to it as his arms pulled her up so she could wrap her legs around him. They moved, and she could feel the cool tile of the shower against her back. Opening her eyes, she saw the silent question in Asher's eyes. "Yes," She whispered, and kept her eyes open as he guided himself inside of her.

The heat inside Hannah threatened to burn him alive, and Asher loved it. How could it feel so good? He didn't know, didn't care, he only wanted her, all of her. "God, Hannah," He said against her lips.

"I know," Hannah answered, not being able to form a coherent thought as he moved inside of her. His hands were cupping her bottom and holding her against him. She would've thought she was too heavy for him to hold, but he held her as if she weighed nothing. And, he filled her so completely. She wondered if she would ever feel this way again. "Yes," Hannah sighed as she felt her body tighten up.

Asher could feel her body tense and prayed she was on the verge of her release because his was coming fast. "Hannah?" He asked her, trying to hold back to make sure she was joining him.

Hannah grabbed onto Asher's shoulders, her body took over, knowing what it needed to find, "Yes, Asher, yes, harder baby," She ground out the words, not even knowing where they came from.

Following her command, Asher drove into her, harder. The clutches of his orgasm were right at the edges of his consciousness and he was trying to hold off. "Hannah," His voice was raised.

The crest of feelings were too much for Hannah, she had no choice but to let them take her over, "Yes," she answered breathlessly, "let it go, baby." Her orgasm was already clawing its way through her body.

With one more thrust, Asher allowed his release to come, and held Hannah tight against him. Her body shook, so he tightened his hold on her.

She saw stars, actual stars! Hannah couldn't even open her eyes for a bit. She felt Asher shift so he could hold her even tighter, and she grabbed onto him.

When Hannah didn't speak for a few minutes, Asher started to worry. He moved so he could look into her eyes, and asked her, "Are you alright?"

'No!' Hannah wanted to shout at him. She was forever changed by him. This……..this lovemaking was more than she ever could have known. "I'm fine," She finally murmured.

Slowly, and with great care, Asher set Hannah down. He turned so she was now under the stream of hot water. Picking up the washcloth he set down earlier, he used the bar of soap and saturated it with suds. As if he were exploring her body for the first time, Asher washed Hannah.

Since all of her strength was sapped, Hannah allowed Asher to take care of her. He was so gentle, he washed her as if she were a delicate piece of glass. As soon as he washed her shoulders, and rinsed them off, he kissed them. Hannah could feel her body start to stir and tried to fight off the sensations.

They got out of the shower, dried one another off, and then Asher did something Hannah didn't expect. He asked her, "Can I brush your hair?"

The question took her by surprise, but she answered, "Yes."

He led her into the bedroom, guided her down onto the bed and put up his hand, silently asking her to wait. He left the room for a minute, and Hannah wondered where he'd gone.

When Asher came back to the bedroom, he told Hannah, "I just wanted to make sure that Skyler was still sleeping."

Her face blushed, "I'm sorry, Asher," she said, "I forgot she was sleeping and I was loud." It was so weird to talk about this.

"You weren't that loud," Asher said as he put his finger in his ear and pretended he couldn't hear. He got a pillow thrown at him for his efforts. Jumping on the bed, he snagged Hannah around her waist and drew her to him. "I was just teasing you," He started to trail kisses on her shoulder, "you telling me what to do was pretty damn sexy."

Hannah looked at him, unsure. "Really?" She asked him.

Stopping his kisses long enough to look into Hannah's eyes, Asher's grew serious. "Sweetheart, you make me feel like I've never done this before."

Coming from a man who was married, Hannah felt smug. "Well, I can't say I'm that practiced, but I think I could get the hang of it."

She was teasing him, and he loved it. "Well, let's get some practice in then," Asher told her, and captured her lips with his.

They slowly made love again. This time though, there were more detailed exploration of bodies.

Hannah found she loved the feel of Asher's body. He was muscled, but not overly so that she felt as if he'd snap her if he hugged her. His thighs were strong, and she ran her fingertips over them, enjoying seeing the reaction his body had to it. "Do you like that?" She asked.

Looking at Hannah, Asher replied, "Yes, or can't you tell?"

Giggling at his intimate pillow talk, she nodded. "I can tell something," She pretended that she was looking for something, and wrapped her hand around his hardening shaft. "Ahh, I think I can tell now," She teased him.

"Woman," Asher whispered, trying to keep coherent thought while she touched him was difficult, "I think you know darn well what you're doing and feeling."

Releasing him, only long enough so that she could straddle him, Hannah tried to look innocent. "Me?" She asked sweetly, "I'm just exploring."

Seeing Hannah, above him, her hair spread across her shoulders, he thought of a Goddess, surveying her domain. Without asking, he grabbed her hips, to hold them in place, then bucked so he flipped them over. Now she was beneath him, open and ready. "I think I'll give you a lesson in exploring then," He told her.

With a smile on her lips, Hannah answered, "I think I'll be happy to learn."

Sliding into her silky core, Asher had to move slowly. Even knowing that they'd made love before, his body was impatient.

Accepting Asher inside of her, Hannah sighed. He felt so good! It was as if he was made just for her. She started to get fidgety when he didn't start moving right away. Opening her eyes, she saw a look of concentration on his face, and began to worry. She asked, "Asher, are you okay?"

Asher was torn between telling her yes and no. He was okay but if she didn't stop moving, he wouldn't be able to last long, and he wanted to please her. "Just hold still for a few seconds," He said through gritted teeth.

Dawning came over Hannah. "Oh," She teased, and ran her hands up his chest. When her fingertips came to his nipples, she flicked them under her fingernails, "So don't do that?" She asked.

'Sometimes,' Asher thought to himself, 'lessons were difficult.' He gave Hannah a look of skilled determination and started to move inside of her. He plunged into her, hard and fast, until he changed her look of teasing into one of want. "That's right, baby," He told her, not focusing on himself, only her.

In a matter of seconds, Hannah felt her body pulse with the impending collision of an orgasm. "Asher," She whispered.

Seeing her on the edge, Asher finally allowed his own body its freedom to take what it wanted. "Yes, Hannah, yes."

Together, they came crashing into the thunderous seas of release. Both of them laid there for a long time, trying to figure out what just happened.

Chapter 15

Hannah opened her eyes, and saw the sun was just beginning to peak around the drawn curtains of the bedroom. A smile immediately crossed her face. She looked over to find a very awake Asher looking at her. "Good morning," She mumbled into the sheet that covered her.

Smiling at her, Asher returned, "Good morning." She was so cute, seeming so shy after their night of lovemaking. He'd been up for a while, even checked on Skyler, and then came back to bed to watch Hannah sleep. She was angelic, even in sleep, and he thought he'd never tire of looking at her.

Scooting over, Hannah said into the sheet, "I need to use the bathroom and brush my teeth."

Asher nodded, and enjoyed the view of her backside as much as he enjoyed all the other views of her. When the water came on in the bathroom, he laid back and thought about their night together. It was……..something he couldn't describe, not yet anyway. He did know that he didn't want to let Hannah go home today. Even though he and Skyler were checking out tomorrow, it just seemed interminable without Hannah.

Hannah was in the bathroom and was shocked by her appearance. Her lips were swollen, from kissing Asher, she assumed. Her body looked different to her somehow. Quickly brushing her teeth, she opened the door and smiled at Asher as he lay in the bed. "You look a little smug this morning," She told him.

Placing his hands behind his head, Asher answered, "I think you could say that."

Sitting back down on the bed, it occurred to Hannah that she hadn't asked him anything before they made love. "I'm kind of embarrassed to ask this, after the fact," She blushed, "but I'm assuming you're not promiscuous so I don't have to worry about anything right?"

Asher was shocked by her question, it came out of the blue. "Hannah," He sat up and pulled her over to him, "I haven't been with a woman since the divorce." He kissed the top of her head. "I'm just glad that you were smart because I didn't think about birth control."

All of a sudden, Hannah's stomach dropped down to her feet. "Uh," She said, and pulled away from Asher. "I, uh, I'm not," She wrung her hands together and started getting upset, "I'm not on birth control."

"What?" Asher almost yelled. "Jesus, Hannah, we……" He pointed to the bed, "without protection?"

The question was like a giant balloon of tension that hung in the air between them. Hannah started to cry, she was upset. "I'm sorry, I just wasn't thinking."

Mad now, Asher shot back, "Wasn't thinking? Hannah you know how this works," He started pacing, "if I'm not wearing a condom; that means that I'm thinking you're on birth control."

Her anger raged up, and alert, Hannah pointed at him, "I'm sorry, Asher, I've only been taking care of my father for the last eight years until he died, so I didn't really have a whole lot of time to think about birth control!"

Wiping his hand down his face, Asher tried to calm himself. "I'm sorry," He told her, "you're right. We're both adults here, we should've discussed this."

"You know what?" Hannah asked him, "You can discuss it with yourself, I'm leaving."

A feeling of dread ran through Asher's body, "Hannah, please don't go?" He asked her.

Tears were streaking down her cheeks, "You know, this was the first time in eight years that I felt something outside of being a caretaker, and now I feel like a chastised child." She put her hand out when he tried to come around the bed towards her. "No, you don't get to just apologize and kiss and make up," She told him, while she grabbed her clothes and started putting them on. "Maybe this is for the best," Hannah told him, her voice shaking with emotion, "this was just a vacation from our lives anyway, right?"

"Hannah, please?" Asher grabbed his shorts and pulled them up as she left the room. He went after her, "I'm sorry, this just threw me."

Trying to be quiet, because Skyler's bedroom door was ajar, Hannah turned to him and said, "Threw you?" She asked sarcastically. "I've been thrown too, and I'm not doing it again," She said with finality before opening the door and leaving.

Asher knew he couldn't go after her, although that's what he wanted to do. Instead, he went out onto the patio and stood there, watching for her. When he saw her, floors below, Asher felt his heart crack into pieces. Turning around, he was shocked to see Skyler standing in the doorway that led to the patio. She had her hands on her hips, and asked him, "What did you do, Daddy?"

Hannah cried all the way back to the bed and breakfast. She came in the kitchen door, and tried to look happy. Unfortunately, Ms. Hanson had an eagle eye, and asked her, "What happened?"

Tossing her bag onto the floor, Hannah plopped down and dropped her face into her hands, crying.

Shelby walked into the kitchen just in time to see a flustered Ms. Hanson fussing over Hannah. Given that Hannah was crying into her hands, it was pretty obvious that she'd had a fight with Asher. "What did he do?" She asked Hannah.

"More like, what did we do?" Hannah tossed back at them. "We made love, and it was magical, awesome, and all that crap, but then I asked him about being promiscuous and he asked me about birth control, and it all went downhill from there." She dropped her face back into her hands, and cried some more.

Looking at Ms. Hanson, Shelby commented, "Well, that just cleared it all up."

Willa shot Shelby a look, and said, "Stop being sassy." She grabbed a carafe of juice and poured Hannah a glass. "Now," She sat down and took Hannah's hands into her own. "I'm sure nothing was said that can't be fixed."

"What if she doesn't want it to be fixed?" Payton said from the doorway into the kitchen.

The three women looked up at her, nobody saying anything.

Payton came into the room and sat down, "You grabbed on to him because he was alive and you needed to feel alive again."

Ms. Hanson started to say, "Payton, I don't think..." but Payton silenced her with a look.

Looking over at Hannah, Payton said, "We're all hurting. I'm mad as hell that my little girl was taken away from me. But, this is part of it, Hannah, grabbing onto things that help us forget the pain."

Shelby sat back, watching the conversation. She shook her head, and told Payton, "No, Payton, that's not it. Kent has been gone a year now, and I haven't gone and found someone to make me feel "alive" yet. I know what it's like to love someone, and Hannah had that look when she talked about Asher."

"Look?" Payton shot back, raising her voice. "What man is ever there for you?" She was angry, and lashing out, but she couldn't stop it, "Hell, your husband went and died on you!"

Her hand shooting out, Shelby slapped Payton across the face. The "whack" of hand connecting with cheek reverberated through the room. With a low voice, she told the Payton, "My husband loved me and I have to believe that he didn't leave me because he wanted to. Now you quit being a bitch and support Hannah."

No one spoke for a few minutes. The pregnant silence threatened to blow up in the room. Even Willa didn't know what to say, she just stood there, her eyes wide with shock.

Hannah, looked at the three of them, and wanted to break the tension. So, she stood up, announced, "Good talk, thanks girls," and left the room. She smiled when she heard laughter a few seconds later.

After going upstairs to her room, Hannah took a shower. She couldn't help but be reminded of her "shower" last night with Asher, and her body thrummed with remembering. She got out, dried her hair, put it into a braid, and came out into the room. The doors to the patio were open, allowing the sounds of the water to come inside. There was a light breeze that blew the curtains around, as if they were dancing.

Hannah got dressed and left her room to go back downstairs.

She didn't know what to expect when she went into the dining room, and she was glad to see Payton and Shelby laughing while Ms. Hanson play slapped at their hands.

Shelby saw Hannah first, "Thank goodness," she said dramatically, "Ms. Hanson wouldn't let us eat until you came down."

Willa rolled her eyes, "I just wanted you all to make sure things were settled."

Absently rubbing her cheek, Payton smiled, "Oh, Shelby settled me pretty quickly."

Hannah tried not to laugh. "Are you okay?" She asked Payton.

Nodding, Payton answered, "Actually, Shelby probably did what everyone else has wanted to do since Raleigh passed away three months ago."

"Is that your daughter's name?" Hannah asked. She smiled when Payton nodded and took out a picture to hand over. It was of Payton, at a much happier time, with a little girl, not more than two or three. She couldn't help it, Hannah started to cry. "She's adorable, Payton."

Smiling, Payton told them, "She actually looked a lot like her daddy." Memories shown on her face, "He wasn't really a big part of her life, and that was my fault." She started to cry.

Shelby and Hannah stood up and walked around to hold Payton. She cried as they held her, missing her little girl so much.

Willa sat there, watching the three of them. Three women who were so different, except for this excruciating loss they each had.

Asher sat on the beach, watching Skyler play. His mood was sullen, although he tried to hide it from his little girl. He should have known better. Skyler walked over to him and asked, "Are you going to call Hannah?"

Not wanting to lie to his daughter, he told her, "I think I hurt Hannah's feelings and she's mad at me."

Her hands propped on her hips, Skyler looked at her father, and asked him, "What do you tell me when I'm mad?" She smiled, "You tell me to apologize, Daddy."

If only adults were as open and honest as kids. He sighed, and told Skyler, "I'll call her in a little bit, okay?"

Skyler looked at her father, a gleam in her eye. "Daddy, can I use your phone?" She asked him.

Knowing his daughter could be as determined as anyone, and knowing that him mom had showed her how to text, he mentally weighed the pros and cons. Finally, he handed over the phone.

Within a few moments, Skyler handed it back, saying, "Your phone is different than Grandma's, can you make it so I can send Hannah a text?"

Trying not to laugh, Asher nodded, and pulled up Hannah's contact, setting it to text, he handed it back to his daughter.

Hannah was sitting out on the back patio with Payton and Shelby when her phone went off. She tried to ignore it, but her friends had other ideas.

Shelby said, "Just look at it. See what he has to say."

Payton was nodding her agreement, so Hannah pulled out the phone and read it.

Hana this is Skylr. Daddy is sorry. Can you come to the beach?

"Oh," Hannah started to cry, "It's not from Asher, but from Skyler." She handed her phone over so Shelby and Payton could read it.

Payton spoke first, "Aww," she got emotional, "I think it's sweet that his daughter sent it."

More skeptical, Shelby offered, "Or he wanted to emotionally blackmail you."

Giving them both a dry look, Hannah reread the text. "Maybe it's a little of both." She said.

Not one to be manipulated easily, Payton gave some credence to the theory. "Well, no matter what, now there's a little girl involved. And she's the one who you have to deal with."

'Damn!' Hannah swore internally. "My bags are in the car already," She explained.

Ms. Hanson came out of the house, a pitcher of lemonade in her hand, and asked, "Well, you can go home, or go to the beach to see them, which is it?"

The three women thought it was a little scary that Ms. Hanson knew everything that was going on. But, she did have a point!

Planting her hands on the table to push herself up, Hannah told them, "I guess I'm going to the beach." She picked up her phone and texted,

Skyler, I'm sure your daddy is sorry. I'll come down to see you for a few minutes, but then I have to go home.

After sending the text, she waved goodbye to the other women and went down the back lawn that led to the beach.

She walked slowly, thinking about what she was going to say to Skyler and then to Asher. Ms. Hanson told her she didn't have to leave, that she and Shelby and Payton could stay as long as they wanted to, but she needed to get home. Putting it off would only make it harder to figure out what she was going to do.

About fifteen minutes later, she saw them. Skyler was playing with some kids and Asher was watching her, but he looked miserable. His jaw was set stubbornly and, even with his sunglasses on, she could see his grimace.

Since Skyler seemed preoccupied, Hannah decided to speak to Asher first. Lord knew, she didn't want to. It would be easier to just walk away, but just looking at him made her insides twist and turn. She knew that feeling wasn't something a person had every day. He hadn't noticed her yet, so she was able to walk up next to him, before saying, "You look upset."

Asher jumped at the sound of Hannah's voice. He'd been thinking about what he should say to her when she came. Now, he just looked at her, and fell into an abyss of emotions once again. "I, uh," He stood up quickly, wiping the sand from his shorts, "I am."

Rather than staying mad, it seemed much easier for Hannah to just walk into his arms, so she did. And she sighed when his arms clamped around her tightly.

Relief poured through him when Hannah hugged him. "I'm so sorry I was such an ass this morning." He told her.

Hannah hugged him tighter, "You were," she answered, "but I didn't help. I'm sorry."

After being married to his ex-wife, a person who couldn't or wouldn't lose a fight, no matter what, Asher was taken aback by Hannah's apology. "I should have asked beforehand, I know that. I just wanted you so much," He whispered to her.

A tear slipped down Hannah's cheek and she released him enough so she could look up at him. "I wanted you too, I still do."

Her words were like an ignition switch for his libido. One little flip and he was on edge, seething with wanting her. "Sweetheart," He whispered, and leaned down to kiss her.

Hannah allowed him to kiss her, she wanted it too. After last night, she knew things were inexplicably different. Even explaining it to Shelby and Payton, she felt changed.

Asher was still kissing Hannah, when he felt a poke on his leg. He stopped kissing her long enough to look down and see his daughter, standing there and smiling. "I told you she'd forgive you, Daddy," She said.

Picking up his daughter, he held her in one arm and Hannah in the other, and told them, "I think she's forgiven me pip squeak."

Hannah nodded, and tapped Skyler's nose with her finger. "He has you to thank for it too," She told the little girl.

Skyler squirmed to get down, smiled brightly, and then ran over to rejoin her friends.

"Sit with me?" Asher asked Hannah.

She nodded and sat down on the towel next to him. He held her hand on the towel between them, rubbing her fingers with the pad of his thumb. The contact made Hannah's insides flutter. Even with that though, she also knew they needed to talk about the argument. "I know that I should have told you that I wasn't on birth control, but I really just didn't think about it. I was preoccupied."

Blushing a little, Asher understood. "I'd say we were both really preoccupied." He pulled her hand up and kissed it. "I want to keep seeing you Hannah."

Looking at him, Hannah replied, "I want that too."

Chapter 16

Hannah stayed with Asher and Skyler for another hour. She wanted to stay longer but she had to go home and face her life at some point. Being with them helped her because she could look forward to seeing them. She and Asher put their addresses in each other's phone so they wouldn't need to later on.

Calling Skyler over, Hannah knelt down in front of the little girl and told her, "Now, you be good for your Daddy."

Nodding solemnly, Skyler then asked Hannah, "Are you going to come and visit us?"

Smiling, Hannah answered, "Of course, I need to see your room and your house!" She wanted to sound enthusiastic when, in reality, it was sad leaving them.

Skyler gave her a hug, and whispered, "You made my daddy smile again," before letting her go.

It was strange to Hannah that she'd thanked Asher for that exact same thing. After Skyler ran off to play with her friends, Hannah stood and walked the few steps to where Asher stood. She could see her own sadness reflected in his eyes. "Don't try to get me to stay, it would be too easy," She said teasingly.

Asher smiled, he knew he could convince her to stay, but she had to face things back at home, on her own. She'd told him as much and he needed to respect that. "I want you to stay more than anything, but I know what you need to do," He looked away for a second, trying to keep his emotions in check, "but understand that I want to see you so don't go all 'let's take a break' on me, okay?"

Hannah nodded, "Okay, promise." She kissed him one more time. "I'll call you tomorrow night and we'll make plans,"

She told him as she started backing away. As soon as she turned to walk forward, tears slid down her cheeks.

A little while later, back at the B & B, Hannah said goodbye to Shelby, who was also leaving, and Payton, who was leaving the next day. They all exchanged numbers too and promised to get together at least once a week for dinner or to talk. They were a group now.

Giving Ms. Hanson one final hug, Hannah said, "Thank you."

Willa got that a lot, but she felt like it was an actuality where Hannah was concerned. "Don't be a stranger now," She called after Hannah as she got into her car.

The drive home was short since traffic was still light. Hannah sighed as she pulled into the driveway of her house. It looked the same, still white with light blue shutters.

Grabbing her bags from the car, Hannah went inside. After being closed up for nearly a week, she decided the house felt stuffy. She went around and opened up windows allowing the afternoon breeze to come in. It was hot out now, but Hannah felt like she needed the outside to come in, even if only briefly. Here there weren't the breezes coming off the water so it wasn't long before Hannah turned on the A/C and started closing the house back up. She popped over to her neighbors', Richard and Heather's, house to collect her mail and to thank them for getting it for her.

She took the pile into the office and sat at the desk to read through it.

There were quite a few condolence cards, so she noted the names and addresses again so she could send out thank you cards. It was crazy because it didn't feel like only ten days since her father's funeral, it felt more like months. She pulled out the envelope her father left for her, and started to try and make sense of it all.

She grabbed her purse and went down to the bank. Even though she knew all the passwords for the accounts, from paying bills, she needed someone to explain it to her.

After going inside, Hannah spoke to the receptionist, and requested to speak with her father's friend, Steve. She was asked to sit down and wait.

A few minutes later, Steve came out to greet her, "Hannah," he said with a smile.

Hannah followed him down a hallway to his office. He waited for her to sit down, then went behind his desk to take his own seat. "Hi, Steve," Hannah finally said.

"How are you?" He asked, then grimaced, "That's a stupid question isn't it?"

Shaking her head no, Hannah responded, "Actually, I'm good, I took a bit of time away, but now I'm back and I'm trying to get all of Dad's financial affairs in order." She pulled out the financial papers that her father put in the folder, as well as the copies of his death certificate that the funeral home mailed to her while she was in Galveston, and handed them all to Steve.

He took a few minutes to review the papers, then he logged onto his computer and looked at some information before turning to her. "Your parents were smart," He told Hannah, "smarter than most of us. They planned well, saved well, and now you are in a great place, financially speaking." He told her. "Since you were on all of his accounts, they won't be tied up in anything."

A bit relieved, because that's what she thought, she asked Steve a few questions. She wanted to know how much was in her education account. What, if anything, she could use that money for if she decided not to go back to school.

Steve gave her a look, "Now, that's tricky. This kind of account is meant to be spent on education, Hannah. If you withdraw the funds for any other reason, there are huge tax penalties you'll have to pay."

Nodding her understanding, Hannah replied. "I'm planning on continuing my education, Steve, I just wanted to know."

Even though he looked skeptical, Steve nodded back. "Okay," He explained, "So, we need to remove your dad's name from all your accounts and you need to come up with a beneficiary for all of this."

Hannah spent the next thirty minutes going over everything with Steve. He helped her contact the life insurance company as well to get that going. It turned out that her father actually had two accounts, one he opened with her mother, and one he opened through the teacher's union. Hannah also handed him the money she was given in the condolence cards, and asked him to make it out into a cashier's check so she could present it to the coaches for new baseball equipment.

He left for a few minutes and then came back, smiling, and said to her, "Your dad would be so proud of you."

"Let's hope so," Hannah responded. She stood up, shook Steve's hand, and said goodbye.

Once she was back in the car, Hannah took a few minutes to just sit there and let it all sink in.

Her father was gone.

After a few minutes, she started up the car, and hoped that Steve's words, about her dad being proud of her, were true.

She texted Shelby when she got home, saying,

House is lonely. Got some financial stuff out of the way, but it's still weird not having my dad here. How are things there?

A few minutes later she got a reply from Shelby,

Decided to take the job filling in at my friend's gym. You were right, I need to step out and start living again. It's been a year and I know Kent would want me to be happy. Miss you, Ms. Hanson, and hell, even Payton.

Hannah read the text and laughed at the mention of missing Payton. She knew what Shelby meant, the last couple of days they were able to see past Payton's grief to the person she really was. She replied to Shelby's text,

Keep me posted and send pics. I want to see you hopping around with all those little kids. ☺

Shelby replied with only an LOL, so Hannah put her phone down and started walking through the house.

By the time she was done roaming through the rooms, it was dinner time, and her stomach was grumbling. There was nothing in the refrigerator because she'd cleaned it out before leaving and she'd forgotten to pull something from the freezer so she ended up ordering in pizza. Pitiful? Yes! And Ms. Hanson would be devastated at the depths to which she'd sunk so quickly.

Thinking about the woman who ran the B & B made Hannah smile. Of course, then her thoughts turned to Asher and Skyler. She was waiting for the pizza when she texted him,

Not sure why, but I find myself thinking about you.

She hoped he would get the sarcasm of the text. A few minutes later she heard her phone go off, and smiled,

Perhaps it's my boyish good looks, the fact that I have an adorable kid, or maybe because I rocked your world last night, take your pick.....

It was obvious he understood her meaning. She replied,

A little full of ourselves aren't we?

Asher saw the question and smiled. He was missing her terribly, even Skyler seemed down now. He'd gotten her off to bed, but desperately wished Hannah was here with him. He texted her,

Nope, trying to cover up my feeling of sadness that you're not with me. ☹

Hannah was getting choked up. She typed quickly,

No fair using sad emoticons. That makes it worse. I wish I was there with you. On a good note, my parents were smart and didn't tie up things, financially speaking.

As soon as she'd sent the text, Hannah regretted it. He probably didn't want to know about her financial stuff, and she shouldn't be sharing that with anyone anyway. She waited for his reply, hoping he wasn't upset.

That's a good thing, when my grandpa passed away, his estate was tied up for almost a year because he didn't have a will. It

was crazy, watching my mom and her siblings decide what was what. It wasn't pretty, we'll just say that.

She was thankful that he didn't seem insulted. Wanting to reply, but knowing it was stupid, when she could just call him, she dialed his number.

Asher picked up on the first ring, and said, "I was just thinking the same thing, why text when we can talk?"

Smiling, Hannah replied, "Exactly!"

They talked for an hour, about all sorts of things. The quietness of her house, when he and Skyler were leaving Galveston the next day, and even the weather. By the time they were done, Hannah was ready for bed, having eaten a slice of pizza, then putting the rest in the fridge. She was snuggled into bed, the phone nuzzled against her ear, and finally said, "I should let you get some sleep."

Lying in bed, at the hotel, Asher whispered, "I don't want to sleep, unless you're here with me."

"No fair," Hannah almost whined.

Chuckling, Asher replied, "Sorry, but I told you this would be tough."

Still smiling, Hannah informed him, "Duly noted, now we'll have to hang up so we can both get some sleep. I'll text you as soon as I wake up tomorrow, if that's okay?" She asked.

Now Asher was smiling, "It's very okay. Goodnight, Hannah," he whispered, then disconnected the call.

As Hannah drifted off to sleep, she held her phone in her hand, and smiled at the thought of Asher being the first person she'd text in the morning.

The next morning, Hannah woke up to someone ringing the doorbell. She looked at her phone, and saw it was only a little after eight. Whoever it was, they were going to get an earful from her. When she opened the door, a few minutes later, her face was set in a frown. "What?" She demanded, then stopped short of her planned rant. There, stood a delivery man, with a huge bouquet of flowers. "Oh," Hannah said, her mind clearing from her sleep fog. "Uh, thank you," She accepted the flowers then asked the man to wait for a tip. He waved her off, saying, "It's already been done," and left. Apparently he wasn't as happy to deliver this early in the morning as she was that someone was ringing her doorbell.

Bringing the bouquet into the kitchen, Hannah smelled the fragrances the blooms created and smiled. She didn't think Asher should have gone to the trouble. Picking up the card, she frowned when she saw that the flowers weren't from Asher, they were from Chris. The card read:

Hope your week in Galveston was great. Let's get together.

Chris

Shaking her head, Hannah realized that Chris did see a lot more into their relationship than she did, and he would need to stop. She went back upstairs, grabbed her phone, and dialed Chris' number.

He answered quickly, with a "Hey there, did you get the flowers?"

"I did," Hannah told him, "But Chris, this has to stop. I like you, and you were a Godsend when Dad was sick, but I'm okay, and I don't see you as a boyfriend." She knew it was harsh, but she didn't want to mislead him in any way.

Chris sat in his living room, his anger growing. "I promised your dad I'd take care of you," He informed her.

Sighing, Hannah tried to keep her temper in check, but he was making it difficult. "I know what Dad said, Chris, and he was worried, but I'm okay."

"I get it," Chris shouted, "You don't want me."

It was a slippery slope, but Hannah knew she had to be straight with Chris. "I don't want you," She said quietly. The phone line disconnected and Hannah hoped this was the last she would hear from Chris about it.

By the afternoon, Hannah had been online paying the monthly bills, and ordering some new living room furniture. The room was empty, except for a few accent tables that were passed down from her grandparents. She'd meant to ask her Aunt Ruth if she wanted them, otherwise Hannah planned on painting them to brighten them up and re-purpose them.

She heated up some leftover pizza and took a roast out of the freezer to thaw. Somehow cooking a big roast, just for herself, seemed silly. It was earlier than she planned to call Asher, but she wanted to speak to him.

Asher had just let Skyler go next door to play with the neighbor's kids, when his phone rang. Seeing it was Hannah, he smiled, and picked up, "Hello there, I didn't expect to hear from you until later."

Feeling bad, Hannah asked, "Is this a bad time? Am I a stalker?"

Chuckling, as he walked through the house, Asher replied, "No, especially since you were supposed to text me this morning, and you didn't. I've been sulking all day."

"Oh geez, I'm sorry," Hannah told him, "I received a huge bouquet of flowers today from a guy that thinks we should date. I don't agree, and I made that very clear."

His male pride getting jacked up, Asher asked her, "Who is it? Do I need to come down there?"

Just hearing him being protective of her, made Hannah happy. "I think he got the message loud and clear, but I'll keep you posted."

Still worried, Asher said, "Call me, day or night if this jackass bothers you."

"I will," Hannah assured him. "And I thank you for being so sweet." She wanted to change the subject and asked him, "How's Skyler?"

His mind still focused on this guy who was bothering Hannah, it took Asher a few seconds to refocus. He smiled, and told her, "Oh, she dumped me already for the seven year-old neighbor boy. They were happily making mud pies when I left her over there."

It was nice, discussing the everyday things. Somehow, that made her feel closer to him. "Well, I called because of a roast."

"Interesting," Asher replied, confused.

Hannah smiled, "Well, I took this roast out, and I can't possibly eat it all by myself, soooo, I was kind of wondering if I could make it and bring it up to your place say, tomorrow?"

That was the best idea Asher had heard all day. "I think that sounds pretty cool." He said, then asked her, "Are you sure you want to see my lair?"

Giggling at his inflection, Hannah answered, "I think I can handle it, super hero."

Now Asher laughed. "I don't know if I'd use the expression super hero, perhaps maybe.......super cool dad?"

"We'll see," Hannah replied, "that depends on what kind of wine you ply me with when I bring up the roast."

His mind calculating, Asher said, "Just be here tomorrow, at six, and we'll see what we'll see."

They hung up a few minutes later, Hannah's brain hazy with luscious thoughts of the "super cool dad."

Chapter 17

That night, Hannah slept fitfully. She wasn't sure if it was the anticipation of seeing Asher the next day, or the stress of getting the flowers from Chris, but her mind just would not shut down.

When her alarm went off the next morning, she shut it off and went back to sleep.

And then, for the second day in a row, she was woken up by the doorbell. Swearing under her breath, Hannah made her way downstairs and was about to yell at the person at the door. That was, until she opened it up to see two delivery guys standing there, smiling. Oh crap! "You're here with the living room furniture, aren't you?" She asked them.

Still smiling, the younger of the two men replied, "Yes, ma'am."

Now she just felt awful. She was standing in her pajamas, thank goodness they were decent and covered her, and getting mad at the guys she requested deliver her furniture this morning.

Running upstairs, she managed to throw on some sweatpants, a t-shirt, and slip into flip flops before the guys got the sofa inside.

"Where do you want it," One of the guys asked, already sweating from the summer heat and humidity.

Hannah pointed, and the guys put the sofa down. They made three more trips, getting the two overstuffed chairs, and the coffee table she ordered.

After they left, Hannah sat down on her new sofa, and smiled. The new, larger furniture made the room feel warmer. It also made the room hers. For the first time, since her dad passed away, Hannah thought of the house as hers, not her parents'.

Asher woke up, and smiled. Hannah was coming over tonight! He'd just seen her two days ago, but it seemed like forever.

His mom was picking up Skyler tonight so she could "bond with her granddaughter" for the week. His parents were great with Skyler, and Asher was thankful for all of their help since the divorce. Thinking of his ex-wife, even in the outer edges of his consciousness, made his smile disappear. Stella Kelley was brilliant, beautiful, determined, successful, and about the coldest person Asher had ever met. She was the opposite of him so he supposed that's why he was drawn to her, at first.

He got up and poured himself a cup of coffee, and leaned on the kitchen counter. Allowing the thoughts of Stella in was still difficult. She'd been so sweet and supportive of his career, as long as it didn't interrupt hers. After Skyler came along, things went downhill fast. Suddenly, there were job opportunities that took her away for weeks at a time. And, when she was home, she wasn't there for him or for Skyler, she was always focused on her next promotion. He tried to make it work, for Skyler's sake, but finally she told him about her current assignment to South America and that she didn't want him or Skyler to go with her.

Their divorce was amicable, probably because she didn't want anything from him. Her income was a lot higher than his and she was more than happy to pay child support for Skyler. She even paid off their house, which still made Asher wonder how she'd gotten that much money. At the time, though, he was just relieved to be done with it.

Now, with Hannah, things looked better. His life seemed brighter. And he really didn't want to screw that up. It was a Blessing that Skyler adored Hannah, and so he didn't have to worry about that aspect of their relationship. When his parents and friends told him he needed to start dating again, he'd resisted, mostly because of not wanting to confuse Skyler.

Just then, the subject of his worry showed up in the doorway of the kitchen. "Hello spud!" He said brightly.

"Good morning, Daddy," Skyler replied as she climbed up onto a barstool in the kitchen.

Asher smiled, walked over to her, and gave her a kiss on the forehead. "What can the chef make you for breakfast this morning?" He asked his little girl.

Sitting there, Skyler gave it some thought, and finally announced, "Pancakes!"

He nodded, and went to the pantry to get out the pancake mix. Even though he only added water to the powder, Skyler thought he made them from "scratch." Feeling a little spunky, he asked her, "How about chocolate chip pancakes?"

Skyler's face lit up, "Oh yes, please," she answered.

If he woke up every day to that smile, Asher knew he'd be a happy man.

Hannah actually did some yoga! She amazed herself, going to the local YMCA and taking a beginner's course. It was all part of her plan of getting out and taking some control over her life. She wanted to focus on her physical and emotional health as if they were one and the same.

The class was hard, and Hannah left the Y in a sweat. She'd chatted with a few of the other women there, and they were very friendly.

She thought about Asher while she was doing the seemingly impossible poses. They'd managed to do some pretty interesting "poses" in his hotel room, and the thought made her smile.

The drive home took less than fifteen minutes, and Hannah showered quickly. She'd put the roast in the crock pot after the furniture delivery guys left, making sure to add onion, potatoes, and carrots. Her mother always told her the seasoning mattered, so she'd put in a few sprinkles of this and that in, hoping it would impress Asher and Skyler.

When she came downstairs, an hour later, the smells coming from the kitchen reassured her she chose well.

Deciding to answer some emails, before calling one of her college friends who demanded they get together soon, Hannah went into the office.

She sat down at the desk, and stopped. For just a second, she thought she felt her dad was nearby. It was fleeting, but the feeling was there. Smiling, she turned on her computer, and waited for it to boot up.

Unfortunately, her email inbox was really full. She was glad that people wanted to communicate with her, but by the time she was halfway through answering, she saw it was already mid-afternoon. She called her college friend while she was turning the roast in the crock pot and they made arrangements to get together for lunch next week.

Mentally calculating traffic, she knew she'd have to leave in about an hour, to get to Asher's house in time for dinner. She had enough time to answer a few more emails.

As she got down to the last couple, Hannah saw one from Ms. Hanson. The subject said Galveston Retreat. Opening it, Hannah smiled.

Dear Hannah:

I wanted to just check on you. I guess it's the mom in me, but I worry about you girls. I know you're not girls, you're grown women who can take care of themselves, but I hope you'll allow me this indulgence. I've been caretaker here for a few years now, and I've never had three guests like you. I want you to know that you're welcome back here anytime you want.

Love,

Willa

By the time Hannah finished reading the email, she was crying. Ms. Hanson had a way with words; that was for sure. She picked up her phone and texted Shelby and Payton in a group text,

I just received the sweetest email from Ms. Hanson at Galveston Retreat. It made me cry. Payton how are you? Do you need anything?

After she sent the text, Hannah went upstairs to put on some light makeup and find a way to tame her hair. She loved that it was long, most days, but sometimes there was so much of it that she didn't know what to do with it. Deciding a French braid was the best, she started the process. By the time she was done, twenty minutes later, her arms were aching, but her hair was up and looked good.

She went back downstairs, to get the crock pot, when she noticed her phone on the counter. She'd forgotten to take it upstairs. There were texts on it so she read them,

(From Shelby) I got one too & yep I cried. She is so sweet. I start teaching my gymnastics classes tomorrow. I'm a little nervous. Payton, if you need us, we're here.

(From Payton) After your text, I checked my email and she got me too. Just when I thought I didn't have any more tears. I'm good, thanks in large part to the two of you. I went into Raleigh's room today, I didn't touch anything, but that was the first time I went in there. I was okay.

Hannah read the texts and was smiling. She was happy that her new friends were doing okay. They were all standing on a precipice of sorts. They had to make the jump back into the living world, and it wasn't always easy. She responded to the texts,

Small steps, Payton. We're proud of you! (I'm just speaking for you Shelby, sorry.) I'd tell you to break a leg, Shelby, on starting your new job, but I don't think we want that, right?

She put the phone down, and got the crock pot secured with a towel, and then took it out to the car. She wanted the food to stay warm, but didn't want the car to be stifling. Oh well, they might have to turn it back on for a bit, but that was okay. By the time she came back inside, to grab her purse, she saw more texts,

(From Shelby) I'll let you speak for me this one time, Hannah, but that's it. ☺ Payton, I agree with Hannah. Small steps...... it takes however long it takes. There's no time limit here. And, HELL NO, we don't want any broken legs!!!!!!!!!! I can't stress that enough!

Hannah laughed as she picked up her phone. After grabbing her purse, she went out to the car. Just as she got in, she heard her phone go off, and read the text,

(From Payton) You two are going to be my comic relief, I just know it. It's been three months, and this was the first time I went into her room. I'll do as you say, but there's something that's nudging me (metaphorically speaking) to start to heal. Thank you both for helping with that.

Reading the text, Hannah's chest tightened. She couldn't imagine what they were going through. Even though her dad was sick for so long, at least they knew the outcome. And, logically, Hannah understood that everyone dies, but to have it happen suddenly, as in Shelby's case, or over only a few months, in Payton's case, that was something she couldn't fathom. She sent one last text before she put the car in gear,

Payton, we (Shelby and I) know how deep the hurt goes, we have your back.

(From Shelby)☺

Putting her phone in her purse, Hannah decided to focus on driving to Asher's house.

An hour and a half later, she was pulling into a beautiful residential area. She knew her house was nice, but it was older and in a more established part of Alvin, Texas. This.......this was a planned community of estates. As she followed her GPS, Hannah started to get nervous. What if Asher was too good for her?

Rolling her eyes at her own dramatics, Hannah shook off her nerves and took a deep breath. If he didn't want to be with her, he certainly wouldn't have invited her up to his house.

Skyler was the lookout! She sat on the living room sofa, anxiously watching for Hannah. Asher would go into the room, periodically, and she would motion him to leave. SHE wanted to be the one who went out to meet Hannah. He'd just left the room, when he heard Skyler yell, "She's here, she's here!" Asher could hear her running for the front door and wished he could show his excitement as easily as his six year-old daughter could.

Hannah pulled into the driveway of a beautiful looking house, and saw Skyler run out the front door. A smile immediately filled her face, and her heart. Skyler's pony tails were flipping as she ran and she looked so excited.

As Hannah got out of the car, she was saying, "Hey there, Skyler!"

Skyler suddenly threw herself into Hannah's arms, hugging her tight. "We've missed you," She whispered into Hannah's ear.

Still holding Skyler, Hannah looked over to see Asher coming out of the house. Lord, he looked wonderful! Hannah kept holding Skyler, and smiled at him, mouthing, "Hi."

When Asher came out, he saw his daughter practically attacking Hannah. It was cute, but he felt bad for Hannah having to extricate Skyler before he could give her a hug and kiss.

A minute later, Skyler saw her friend from next door, come out into the yard, and released Hannah. She looked at Asher, and asked, "Daddy, can I go and play, please?"

Asher nodded, and watched his daughter take off across the front yard, and into the neighbor's. He turned around and found himself face to face with Hannah. Oh, she looked lovely. She'd braided her hair so it was off of her face, but wrapped the ends of the braid up so it looked intricately placed at the nape of her neck. He stepped closer, and took her into his arms. "Finally," He said, then kissed her.

The kiss was light, a hello kiss, but it did crazy things to Hannah's chest. She had a difficult time breathing for a good minute, and just stood there smiling at him. She felt the same way. Realizing, she left the roast on the floor of the back seat, Hannah moved quickly to pick up the crock pot.

Stepping closer, Asher took the pot from Hannah and asked her to, "Come on in."

Just behind Asher, Hannah got her first look at his house. It was huge! Probably twice the size of hers. "Your house is spectacular," She said.

Shrugging, Asher looked at the house for a moment, then responded, "Yeah, I guess so."

Surprised by his nonchalant answer, Hannah just decided to go with it. They walked inside and she gasped. The house was actually larger on the inside than it appeared to be on the outside. The foyer was two stories tall, accommodating a rounded staircase to the right side of it.

They walked down the hallway, and Hannah could see doors here and there, but didn't dare ask where they led. She was practically drooling when she saw his kitchen. It was a chef's dream! All the appliances were state-of-the-art and it was so roomy with, what appeared to be, miles of counter space. "Oh my, Asher, this is fantastic!"

Even knowing that the house was grand, on most peoples' scales, he'd just lived here and didn't pay much attention. "I'm glad you like it," He told Hannah, unsure what she might think of it.

"I'll only like it if you let me cook for you here," She told him as she wrapped her arms around his waist, "and if you give me the kiss I'd like you to give me."

Well, the first thing, he surely wouldn't mind because he didn't use half the stuff in the kitchen, and the second, well that would be his pleasure. He placed the crock pot on the counter then proceeded to bring his head down to meld his lips with hers.

As soon as Asher's lips met hers, Hannah sighed in contentment. Her arms tightened around him, and she opened her mouth to deepen the kiss.

Asher felt like he'd just been lifted up into the air, and held suspended. Her response to his kiss was eager, and that drove his need into a whole new arena of awareness.

The front door closed, and the noise of it had Asher and Hannah stepping apart as if they were caught.

"Hello?" Came a voice from the entryway.

After taking a deep breath, to calm his raging hormones, and prepare himself, Asher returned, "In here, Mom."

All Hannah could think was 'Mom?' Her palms grew sweaty and her heart sped up, but for a whole new reason now.

Brenda Kelley came into her son's kitchen, and stopped immediately. There was a pretty woman in there with him, an unusual sight since the divorce. But, even more unusual, was the look of being caught that both her son and this mysterious woman wore on their faces. Regaining her bearings quickly, Brenda smiled, and said, "Oh, hello."

Moving around the counter, Asher went over to give his mom a hug. He smiled, and said, "Mom, this is Hannah," he looked at Hannah, and added, "Hannah, this is my mom, Brenda Kelley."

Holding out her hand, as she was moving toward Hannah, Brenda told her, "Just call me Brenda," she held the young woman's hand gently. "Hi, Hannah."

Asher's mother was so welcoming that Hannah couldn't help but smile. Her son obviously inherited his mother's ability to put people at ease. "Hello, Mrs., er Brenda." She murmured.

Oh, this lady was a stunner. Brenda wanted so badly to sit down and ask the millions of questions that were on the tip of her tongue but, one look from her son told her now was most definitely not the time for interrogations. She just replied, "It's nice to meet you," she sniffed, "and what smells so good?"

Smiling, Asher told his mom, "Hannah made a roast today and brought it up for us to eat for dinner." He knew he was rolling the dice in asking, but he did anyway, "Mom, do you want to stay and eat with us?"

Hannah was surprised at Asher's impromptu invitation to his mom. Not that she minded. Mrs. Kelley seemed very sweet.

Waving her hand to her son, Brenda answered, "I can't. I'm simply here to pick up my granddaughter and spoil her for the next week."

Looking from Asher, to his mother, and then back to him, Hannah didn't say anything. She got the feeling though, that there was definitely information going back and forth between mother and son.

The front door slammed, and there was a muted, "Sorry, Daddy," shouted from Skyler. The adults heard footsteps run up the stairs, stop for a few moments, and then come back down the stairs. Skyler appeared in the doorway, next to her father, and announced, "I'm ready to go, Grandma."

Smiling at Hannah, Brenda said, "I hope I'll see you again, Hannah."

"Oh yeah, Grandma, Hannah is Daddy's new girlfriend." She smiled brightly, "She even stayed overnight at our hotel when we were on vacation."

If the floor could open up and swallow her and Hannah would've welcomed it. She looked at Asher, her eyes wide, and he just sighed.

Brenda's eyebrows rose, she clapped her hands together, and said, "Okay," she smiled at Hannah one last time, and walked toward her son, "you can tell Grandma all about it," was directed at Skyler as they walked out of the house.

When the front door closed again, Asher's shoulders dropped. "I'm so sorry, Hannah."

Hannah couldn't help it, she started to laugh.

Chapter 18

Asher was thinking many things right now, but laughing wasn't among them. Hannah did look adorable, laughing in his kitchen, so he just let her be.

"I'm sorry," Hannah finally said to him. "It was just too precious, the look on your mom's face when Skyler told her about our sleepover."

Smirking, Asher walked over to where Hannah was standing, and pulled her into his arms. "You know that I'm going to be raked over the coals, a bright light shined into my eyes, and possibly even beaten with rubber hoses until I tell her everything about you."

Just the mental image of what he described made Hannah laugh some more. "Can I watch?" She asked, and then darted away from him.

Getting the game, Asher ran after her, snagging her around the waist and pulling her up against him. He kissed her neck so she stopped laughing, and lifted up her hands to hold him in place.

They were now in the family room, much less formal than the rest of the house. Here is where Hannah could see the real Asher. Skyler's toys were here and there, wherever she left them, there was a princess blanket on the sofa, and children's DVD's on the shelf. She sighed as he kept kissing her neck, and finally said, "If you don't stop that, you'll miss dinner."

Pulling away from her, Asher tried to look torn between choosing food and her. He would look at the kitchen, then to her, and then back to the kitchen.

Thinking he was a brat, Hannah playfully slapped his arm, and told him, "Let's get in there and eat the roast."

Pretending to be dragged, Asher replied, "Okay, if I have to."

Luckily, the roast stayed pretty warm during the drive. They were able to serve it quickly, and decided to sit out on the back patio. There were ceiling fans installed in the rafters that covered the patio so the breeze they created made the heat bearable.

Asher took the first bite, and gave Hannah a look, before commenting, "Oh, woman, you can cook!"

She chuckled, and replied, "I sure hope so, otherwise you may not ask me to come back."

"I may not let you leave," Asher commented, then stopped when he realized how that sounded. "I didn't mean that in a creepy, serial killer kind of way."

Hannah laughed, "Not taken that way, actually it gave me other, more interesting ideas."

Her tone had his mind moving away from the food, and toward a more primal appetite. "Really?" He asked, drawing out the word.

Leaning back in the chair, Hannah asked him, "Not to kill the mood, but did you live here with your ex-wife?"

The question did throw some cold water onto his libido, but he understood why Hannah would ask it. "We bought the house right after Skyler was born. I think Stella stayed here a total of about six months in five years, give or take."

'Her name is Stella,' Hannah made a mental note to herself. "She traveled that much?" She asked.

Mimicking Hannah, Asher leaned back in his seat. He didn't really want to discuss his ex-wife, but Hannah had questions, and he wanted to be honest with her. He responded, "She avoided us that much," he couldn't quite keep the contempt out of his tone as he spoke.

Knowing she'd hit a nerve, Hannah was reluctant to ask more, but she wanted to know things. "Did you pick out the house?" She asked him.

Asher shook his head, "Hell no," he told Hannah, "Stella thought it 'made a statement' so we bought it." He looked at Hannah, and added, "I'm an eighth grade History teacher, do you think I could afford this place, no!" He tried to lighten his tone by saying, "But she paid it off as part of the divorce settlement so I stayed. It's a great school system, and Skyler is happy here."

"So, would it bother you if we made love in your bed here?" Hannah asked him. She was feeling bold, and he was obviously over his ex-wife.

It was like Hannah just flipped a switch inside of him. A few words and he felt like a randy teenager. "No, Hannah, it wouldn't bother me in the least," He looked at her, and asked, "Would it bother you?"

Taking a moment to think about it, Hannah slowly smiled, and responded, "Hell no, her loss is most definitely my gain." She moved to stand up, then stopped, looked at Asher, and told him, "But, I haven't gone to the doctor yet to get birth control, and it didn't occur to me to pick up condoms before I got here."

How could a conversation about condoms make him so crazy with need for her? He didn't know, and frankly, Asher didn't care. He stood up too, and replied, "It's a good thing I picked some condoms up earlier today, when I was shopping."

They walked back into the kitchen to clean up the plates and put the leftovers away. Even though they both wanted intimacy, there was no hurry tonight. Skyler was with her grandparents and they had the whole house to themselves.

Asher found he liked having Hannah here, in the house. The rooms felt warmer, homier, when she was in them. He forgot how lonely he was before she came into his life. Or maybe he just hadn't realized it.

"You're quiet, are you thinking?" Hannah asked him, as they put the dishes back into the cupboard.

He nodded, and answered, "I was thinking how much I like you being here, in the house."

Standing a foot from him, her hands on her hips, Hannah replied, "Well, if your charm and handsome good looks wouldn't have gotten me to sleep with you, then that comment certainly would have."

They talked, and stayed close as they moved through the house, making sure that lights were turned off and doors were locked for the night. It was as if they'd been doing it for years rather than just this once. Hannah told him about her email from Ms. Hanson, and her texts with Shelby and Payton. He told her about Skyler's antics and his prep week for the next school year, which was coming up next month.

Within minutes, they were upstairs in Asher's bedroom.

Hannah walked around the room, looking at things, touching a picture of Skyler, from when she was a baby, and running her fingers over a wooden box on his dresser. This was all Asher, all a part of the private man. She was curious to see and to feel and to know this part of him.

Asher watched Hannah move around his room. He wanted her to feel comfortable. It felt a little like she was getting to know him in a different way. "Do you like what you see?" He asked, his tone plainly suggestive.

Standing beside his bed, Hannah looked at him, "I do," she answered, and sat down on the soft comforter.

He slowly walked over to where she sat on his bed, and sat down beside her. Cupping her cheek with the palm of his hand, Asher whispered, "I'm glad," and leaned over to kiss her.

This was something different than the other night, at least in Hannah's mind. This was a slow, steady burn rather than a quick flash of heat. She took her time kissing him, exploring his mouth as if it were unfamiliar territory. She wanted to be the person who kissed him senseless. Lord knew, he did that to her.

Shifting, Asher pulled her onto the bed beside him. They were still fully clothed, but the kisses were building in their intimate momentum.

Hannah allowed herself to let go. She started yanking at his shirt, to get it off, and once that was done, she was groping for the button on his jeans. The heat inside of her threatened to consume her, and she knew having Asher inside of her was the only thing to sate it. "More," She growled against his mouth.

Asher smiled, she was demanding, and he loved that about her. He returned the favor and peeled off her shirt, made quick work of unhooking her bra, and pushing down the skirt she wore, along with her panties.

When they were naked, Hannah made sure they were touching, from their intertwined legs up to their locked lips. The sensations of his body, strong and hard, against hers, soft and giving, made her pulse run wild. She wanted to be in control so she moved over a bit, then straddled him. She felt his hardness against her clit and wanted to cry out then. Rubbing back and forth, she reached up to undo her braided hair.

Asher was beneath her, and watched her, as if she were a piece of art he was trying to figure out. Her body, tanned and supple, moved against him. She probably didn't know how much the movement drove him crazy, but he didn't say anything as she released her hair. The tresses fell down over her shoulders, with strands of the soft gold whispering across his skin as she leaned down to kiss him. He used one hand to reach over into the nightstand, and grabbed a condom out of the box. His hands shook as he tried to tear it open, causing Hannah to giggle. "Hey, I'm new at this," He told her, and finally got it out of the wrapping. Sheathing himself, he lifted her slightly so that she could settle on him, her softness taking him in. The torture was beautiful.

Hannah wasn't sure what they'd done to condoms but this one felt soooooo good. Maybe it was the fact that she was on top of Asher, looking down on him, and he was so deep inside of her. It didn't matter what caused it, but the pleasure was so immense, that she wanted to cry out. "Oh, yes," She told him, her breath coming faster with their increasing rhythm.

Hearing Hannah talk as they made love was something that drove him to the brink of release in no time. "Yes, baby," He returned, hoping to stave off his release until she had hers.

She could see the look of concentration on Asher's face. He was ready to cum, and yet, she wanted more. She moved faster, riding him wildly. Her orgasm flew up on her, and took her body by surprise with its intensity. She watched as Asher bucked upward, allowing his own to take him into the maelstrom of release.

They laid there, on top of the comforter, for a while. Asher leisurely running his fingers up and down her side. She was tucked tightly against him, her head on his chest, and listened to his heart beat. The steadiness of it lulled her to sleep.

Asher felt Hannah drift off, and wanted to follow her into the pleasantness of slumber, but his mind wouldn't allow it. He was in love! With Hannah! And although he wasn't sure, he thought she most likely wasn't in love with him, not yet. She had a lot of decisions to make in the coming weeks and months and he didn't want to influence her in any way with words of love.

She shifted, cuddled closer to him, and then settled again.

He watched the darkness of the evening come, and tried to figure out how to love her and give her the space she needed to find her own way. The two things were in direct contradiction.

When Hannah woke up, she was alone. It took her a minute to remember that she was at Asher's house, and in his bed. The memory of the night before made her smile. She imagined most women smiled that way when they felt sated physically by a man. The only problem Hannah could see right now, was that it wasn't just physical for her. She was invested now, with Asher and Skyler, and she had absolutely no idea how to do the "casual dating" thing. Before she could come up with any answers, she saw the bathroom door open, and a smiling Asher coming out.

"Good morning," Asher said to Hannah as he exited the bathroom. When he did finally fall asleep, he slept deeply. Hannah soothed him. He woke up rested and ready for the day, so he slowly got out of bed, careful not to wake her, and jumped in the shower.

Hannah smiled, "Good morning." She felt a little self-conscious since she hadn't brought anything with her. "Uh, I didn't even bring a brush or a toothbrush with me," She told Asher.

Pointing toward the bathroom, Asher replied, "I have both set out for you." He felt he needed to explain, and said, "The brush is an extra one for Skyler, and the toothbrush is an extra one for me." He leaned over, and kissed her forehead. "You go on in, I've got towels set out, and even a hair clip if you don't want to wash your hair, and I'll meet you downstairs when you're done." He walked over to his dresser, and started pulling out clothes.

Making a beeline for the bathroom, Hannah felt strange, and she couldn't figure out why.

Thirty minutes later, she was coming downstairs. Asher had laid her clothes out on the bed nicely, and she should be grateful, but she just felt off kilter somehow. He was standing at the stove, cooking, when she came into the kitchen.

"Was your shower okay?" Asher asked Hannah over his shoulder. When she nodded yes, he looked back at the pan. "I hope you like scrambled eggs because that's the only type of eggs I can seem to make."

Smiling, Hannah watched him. He moved so smoothly, for a man. She hated using the word glide because it sounded girly, but he did, he just sort of glided around. "Thank you," She told him when he placed the plate in front of her.

They ate in silence. The wonderful easiness of the night before was gone. Asher felt it now, and asked Hannah, "Are you alright?"

Hannah turned toward him. "You know, I'm not." She answered truthfully, and hoping he would understand. "And the problem is, I don't know why."

He was glad she was honest, but upset because there was no clear answer. "Did I do something?" He asked.

Shaking her head no, Hannah told him, "You made me feel so good, so beautiful last night."

Leaning over to kiss her, Asher drew out the kiss, because he feared they were losing some newly gained emotional ground.

When he kissed her, it was easy for Hannah to be lulled into the magic of the chemistry between them. It was very powerful, but she needed a clear head in order to figure out what was going on with herself. "You are very good at that," She informed him after ending the kiss.

A gleam in his eye, Asher whispered, "I can do it again, you just need to say the word."

Oh, how she wanted to. She wanted to do everything, over and over again, with him. It would be so easy to just fall into that maze of sexual exploration. Asher was a giving lover, she could see that right away, and she would never get tired of making love with him. But something, something in her gut, just told her to slow down, and back off. "I think I'm going to get going," She said as she took her plate over to the sink.

She was leaving? Asher didn't expect that whatsoever. "Why?" He asked.

"I don't know," Hannah told him.

Now Asher's frustration was getting the better of him. "You're not okay, but you don't know why, and you're leaving, but you don't know why. Is there anything you do know?" He spat out the words in an accusatory tone.

Hannah wasn't expecting this kind of backlash to her telling him she was leaving. "Well, I do know that I'm very offended by your controlling and condescending tone," She shot back quickly.

Even knowing that he was navigating a verbal mine field, Asher couldn't quite keep himself from saying what he knew darn well he should not say, "Fine, then go!" As soon as the words passed his lips, he knew they were the wrong ones. "Hannah," He started to apologize, but he could see the damage was done.

Her tone was calm, because if she didn't remain calm, she would punch him, "I would appreciate if you never spoke to me like that again."

"Hannah, I'm sorry," Asher said quietly.

It was too late, she was angry, and she knew they were both too sensitive and their relationship too new to figure this out rationally. "I'll call you when I do know something," She told him, grabbed her purse, and left the house.

Asher stood in his kitchen, cursing himself twenty different ways for being such an ass.

Hannah got home in an hour. She pulled into the driveway, and finally let the tears come as she put the car in park. Her father always told her not to drive when she was upset, but she figured he'd give her a pass on this one. "Oh, Dad," She said aloud, "where are you when I need you?" With no answer, Hannah got out of the car and went into the house.

She went into the office, and threw her purse onto the desk. Her phone half fell out, and Hannah could see texts on the screen so she picked it up, they were from Asher,

Hannah, I'm an ass, I'm so sorry. I know you probably won't see this until you're home, but PLEASE text me when you get there so I know you made it safe.

Feeling torn, Hannah had to wait a few minutes before deciding whether to text him or not. In the end, she figured she shouldn't act like a jerk, just because he was, so she texted her response,

I'm home.

When Asher got the text he was relieved, and then he was even more worried because a woman who said very little, was saying a whole helluva lot.

Chapter 19

Asher knew his mother would call him. He knew she would "summon" him over to their house. And she called him a few hours after Hannah left.

"Hello, son," Brenda Kelley greeted her son when he answered his phone.

He couldn't help it, he was being a jerk, and replied, "Mom, I'm not in the mood."

'Well, that statement spoke volumes,' Brenda thought to herself. "Do you want to come over tonight for dinner?" She asked, cutting to the chase.

Sighing, Asher asked, "What time?"

The day seemed to last forever, in Hannah's dramatic brain anyway. It was only six o'clock. Only eight hours since she saw Asher, and she missed him like crazy. "Well, then maybe you shouldn't have said you were leaving," She said aloud, to herself.

She'd gone over every minute of her time at his house and could not come up with anything that should have made her feel unsettled. Yet, that's exactly what she was feeling. Maybe they needed some space? Maybe they needed a little time to figure out what all of this meant. Maybe she was having some sort of break down and needed to see a psychologist?

Pacing the length of the office, she wondered, for the gazillionth time what was wrong with her. She looked up and saw a picture of her father and her, and walked over to pick it up.

Running her fingers over the glass that covered the image, Hannah thought about her father. He was wearing his coach uniform and it was just after his team won the state championship. What was it? Ten years ago? Hannah retraced the image with her fingertip, hoping to get some answers from it.

Asher arrived at his parents' house, and sat outside in his car for a good twenty minutes before going inside. He felt he needed a little bit of time to settle down his emotions. With a final sigh, he got out of the car, and walked up to the door. His father met him there, with a smile of pity on his face.

"Hello, son," Henry Kelley said to his son. He knew what the boy was in for, and did feel slightly sorry for him, with an emphasis being on the word slightly. For once, his wife's focus was not on him, and that was just fine with Henry.

Smiling at his dad, Asher replied, "Hey, Dad, how are ya?"

Clapping his son on the back, Henry returned, "Better than you, if what I hear from your mother, and your daughter is correct."

Asher winced at the words. It didn't even occur to him to speak to Skyler about Hannah's involvement in their life. It hadn't been an issue before now, so he was flying blind anyway. He sighed again, and followed his dad through their house.

Brenda and Henry Keller still lived in the house they bought as newlyweds, and raised their children in. It wasn't a fancy place, but it was home, and a place where they always gathered as a family. Asher knew every inch of his parents' house and usually felt comfortable when coming here. Not tonight.

"Asher," Brenda announced, and hung up the phone. She got up from the outside table and walked over to give her son a kiss hello.

Shaking his head, Asher commented, "Conspiring with my sister, I see."

Brenda had the humility to look caught, but only for a few seconds. There were matters she wanted to look into where her son and granddaughter were concerned. "I don't think I'd use the word conspiring, more like consulting."

Asher looked at his father, who was standing behind him now, and they both said, "Conspiring," in unison.

Rolling her eyes, Brenda motioned for her son and husband to join her at the table. She poured them each a glass of iced tea, and then sat back down. "I asked your sister to take Skyler tonight, so we could talk."

Seeing the look on his mother's face, Asher wanted to run away. It was childish, yes, but he was still raw from Hannah's unsettling departure this morning, so an interrogation now wasn't welcomed. "What is it, Mom?" He asked, frustrated.

Brenda looked at her husband and, with only a look, told him that she was worried about their son. "I, uh, just wanted to know what Dad and I could do to help you." She placed her hand over Asher's. "I know dating and taking care of a little girl can get complicated."

This was not what Asher was expecting, so he had to mentally check out for a minute. "Wait a minute," He said to her when he regained his mental footing, "why are you offering to help instead of questioning me about Hannah?"

Now it was Brenda's turn to take a few seconds. "I saw something yesterday, I didn't think I'd see again," She paused and smiled at her son, "I saw you happy, genuinely happy, not just trying to put up a front for Skyler and us."

His mother's words were a surprise to Asher. "I was happy, Mom," he replied, a little defensively.

Now Henry spoke to his son, telling him, "No, you weren't. We saw what Stella's leaving did to you." He put his hand on his son's shoulders, and explained, "You felt rejected and alone."

There were no words that Asher could come up with to refute his parents' arguments, so he just nodded and remained quiet.

"I saw you and Hannah," Brenda explained, "and it was like there was this light that was let into your house, and you." She tried not to cry, "My beautiful boy was feeling better and, as a mother, I was happy for you."

Asher felt a little ashamed now. "Well, I don't know how happy any of us are now. Hannah stayed over last night," He didn't really want to give his parents intimate details, so he skipped over them, "and then this morning, she just said she felt "off." I got mad and pushed her for more of an explanation and she left." He looked back and forth between her parents, before continuing, "And now she won't answer my calls."

Henry leaned forward. "Skyler told us that her dad just died."

Nodding, Asher looked at his father, "It was a long battle with ALS."

His brow furrowed, Henry asked Asher, "What did her father do?"

Thinking for a second, Asher answered, "I think he was a coach at a high school in Alvin."

"Oh, sweet Jesus," Henry said, looking at his wife. "Frank Whitman," He told her, expecting her to remember. He looked at his son to explain. "Frank and I did some work together the summer after he graduated from high school. I was a couple of years older so I kind of took him under my wing."

This was turning into a very strange conversation to Asher. "You knew Hannah's dad?"

Nodding, Henry told him, "Yes, we were both working for the same company, just for the summer. I decided to stay on, and Frank, well, Frank wanted to play professional baseball and was focused on that." He looked like he was miles away, remembering his old friend, "He coached that kid a few years ago, the one who went on to play for the Astros.....what was his name?"

Both Brenda and Asher drew blanks. Neither of them really followed baseball. Asher just shook his head, and said, "Small world."

Still looking a little dreamy, Henry added, "I didn't get a chance to go to his funeral, but I heard a lot of people attended."

Asher nodded to his dad, "Yes, and there were a lot of donations to the family so Hannah is donating them to the high school's baseball program."

Putting her hand to her chest, Brenda started to tear up, "Oh, that's so sweet," she whispered.

"That's how Hannah is," Asher told his mom. "But I went and got all controlling and now she's not speaking to me."

It was hard not to smile at her son's obvious discomfort. "I think if you give Hannah a little time, I think she'll come around." She patted Asher's hand, "Remember, she's just lost her dad, and now she finds you, and Skyler, and her feelings are all out of control." Sighing, she took a quick sip of her tea, and added, "I'll bet she's just confused." Nodding, as if she was sure of her theory, Brenda told Asher, "You see, we're all expected to grieve, and so to find happiness, so soon after her father's death, probably makes her feel guilty."

His mother's words made sense to Asher. He looked over to see his dad lost in thoughts; probably memories of his old friend, and he felt bad for him too. "I'll try to be patient, Mom, I promise."

"Good," Brenda smiled, "Now take us out to dinner because I was too lazy to cook."

Chuckling, Asher thought this was exactly why he loved his parents.

At eight o'clock, Hannah couldn't take the silence anymore. She sent a text to Shelby and Payton,

I'm having a rough night. Had a fight with Asher and I don't even know why. Would you gals mind if we met up tomorrow to talk? I know it's last minute.

After sending the text, Hannah went upstairs to get ready for bed. She flipped on the small television in her room, just to have some background noise, and went into the bathroom to brush her teeth and wash up. When she came out, she saw that the girls had responded.

(From Shelby) I'm free after 3pm, that's when my last class lets out. I'm in Friendswood so we can meet in that area, or elsewhere if you would like. Payton?

(From Payton) I'm open. I was going to call you both to ask if you wanted to get together anyway. A few things I wanted to run by you both and get your take on them. How about Pearland? I'm in Sugarland so that would be about central to all of us.

Smiling, because these women knew she needed them, and wanted to help her. Hannah texted,

How about that new restaurant at the Pearland Town Center, 5pm?

She slipped out of her clothes, and into her pajamas before she heard the phone ping with responses.

(From Shelby) I'm there.

(From Payton) I'll see you both then.

Hannah put the phone on the bedside table and got into bed. She flipped through the channels for a while, wondering what people did. Her life literally was wrapped around her dad's schedule so to have this much "free time" was so weird. "Oh Dad," She said aloud, and let the tears fall down her cheeks.

Asher got home around ten o'clock from taking his parents out to dinner. They lived in Pasadena, which was just to the east of Houston, so getting home took him a bit. He hadn't even seen Skyler because she was at his sister's place in South Houston. The dinner was good and his parents certainly gave him plenty to think about. The fact that his father knew Hannah's dad truly blew Asher's mind away. Before he thought too much about it, he sent her a text,

I had dinner with my parents, my interrogation about you. It turns out our dads knew one another. Crazy huh?

Her phone going off pulled Hannah out of her half sleep. She'd just finally settled down so the intrusion frustrated her. As she read it, though, her mind started waking up.

Really? How is that possible?

She sent the response text and sat there, waiting.

Relieved that she responded, if only in a text, Asher typed,

They worked for the same company the summer after high school. My dad thought a lot of yours, so he wanted me to pass on his condolences.

For some reason, Hannah began to cry. She wasn't sure if it was because Asher's father, someone she'd never met, was sorry for her father's passing, or because she was just that lonely without her dad here. It didn't matter, the tears were helping her flush out her feelings and that was better than keeping them bottled up inside. She typed back,

Thank you, and thank your dad. I was really missing dad today and this is part of it. I'm sorry we fought. And I'm sorry that I can't give you the answers you want right now. Maybe we're just in different places in our lives.

Her text made Asher frown. He couldn't......no, he wouldn't accept that. There was a reason that they were brought together here and now. The fact that their fathers knew one another solidified that thought. He wanted Hannah to be reassured, but wasn't sure how to do that. He typed,

I don't agree. I believe in things like fate, Hannah. We were supposed to meet now, I know it. I will give you the time and space you need to figure out what you want to do. But know, that we (Skyler and I) are here when you're ready.

Now her tears were really flowing. Hannah felt a mixture of relief and fear that by the time she was ready that Asher would have moved on. She put the phone down, and didn't text back.

The next day, Hannah received an email from Ms. Jasper, the head coach at the high school. Basically, they were having a coach's meeting the following week and wanted to do a remembrance ceremony for her father along with that. The thought touched Hannah deeply and she emailed Ms. Jasper back, letting her know that would be lovely.

The hours of the day dragged by, just like the day before, and she was relieved when it was time to head north to Pearland. Traffic was bearable and Hannah was glad she made good time. She was debating on whether she should text her two friends, when she saw Shelby pull into a parking spot nearby.

Both women got out of their cars, met halfway between, and hugged.

"How are you?" Shelby asked Hannah.

Shrugging, Hannah replied, "I'll tell you when Payton gets here and we can all vent."

Shelby nodded, and they walked inside to wait in the air conditioning.

Payton arrived a few minutes later, hugging both Hannah and Shelby tightly.

Hannah couldn't help but notice the difference in Payton. The angry woman she first encountered in Galveston was almost gone. Replacing her was a beautiful, if not still too skinny, woman who looked……..hopeful.

They were shown to their table, and sat down.

Hannah smiled, saying, "Payton, you look so different."

Shelby nodded in agreement, and demanded, "Spill!"

With a shy smile, Payton answered, "Okay, all I'll say is that I've been in contact with Raleigh's father."

Looking at one another, Hannah and Shelby passed a look of confusion between them, then looked back at Payton expectantly.

"I know, I haven't mentioned him," Payton told them.

Looking a little embarrassed, Hannah replied, "I'm sorry, Payton, I assumed you were married."

Nodding her agreement, Shelby piped up with, "Me too."

Payton nodded to them, "I know, most people make that assumption, but it wasn't the right time for us when I got pregnant with Raleigh. It wasn't a long term relationship and I was so scared about having a baby. He was supportive emotionally and financially, but I'm afraid I pushed him away."

Hannah could understand that. "You've both shared an awful loss," She expressed, and reached over to hold Payton's hand.

"Yes," Payton replied, "and with him feeling as lost as I am, it actually helps."

Shelby commented, "Understandable," and tried not to cry. She still missed Kent, even after a year. It was as if half of her was gone now.

Not sure this dinner was such a good idea, Hannah told Shelby and Payton, "Well, I asked you here because I stayed over at Asher's house the other night, and then I practically ran away, I was so scared."

Intrigued, Shelby looked at Hannah closely, "What were you scared of?" She asked.

"I have no idea," Hannah answered honestly. "It was like nothing fit right and I just couldn't handle it."

Payton leaned forward, and asked Hannah, "Do you think maybe you were torn?" She saw Hannah's questioning look, and told her, "Between understanding what you lost, your parents, and what you may have found with Asher and his little girl, Skyler."

Hannah sighed, "I don't know. I miss him when I'm not with him, and then when I'm with him, I'm so off kilter."

Shelby took a sip of her water, and announced, "Sounds like love to me."

Looking at her friends, Hannah wondered if her friends' thoughts had merit.

Chapter 20

They spent time talking about the loved ones they lost, and caught up on the events of their life now.

Shelby asked Hannah, "Are you going back to school?"

Hannah nodded, "Yes, but I'm not sure what I'll major in. I don't feel like Marine Biology is a good fit anymore but I don't know what I want to do."

Payton said, "I think you'd make a great counselor, if my opinion means anything."

Looking at Shelby, Hannah saw her nodding as well. "Maybe," She looked around, "I don't know."

Winking at Hannah, Payton murmured, "I hear teaching is pretty popular these days," and she winked at her friend.

The meaning of the words weren't lost on Hannah. She would need to think through a lot of things. "By the way," She looked at Shelby, and asked, "How have your classes been going?"

A flush filled Shelby's cheeks, and she looked down at her plate. "Fine," She said quickly.

Now Hannah exchanged glances with Payton, her eyebrows raised. "Oh, there is so much more to that word," Hannah nudged Shelby with her elbow while Payton chuckled.

"Fine," Shelby said more forcefully, "I met an uncle of one of the students, and he asked me out."

Her eyebrows raised, Hannah asked her, "So, what did you say?"

A half smile on her face, Shelby replied, "I said no, but…" her voice trailed off.

Payton picked up the words with, "But….." and looked at Shelby eagerly.

"But, I'm not sure," Shelby replied. "I know it's been a year now, but he's still here," She pointed at her heart.

Hannah nodded, "He always will be, Shelby, that won't change. But, do you think Kent would be upset if you went out?"

Smiling, Shelby answered, "He'd be the first one to demand I go on living." A tear slipped down her cheek.

Leaning forward, Payton whispered, "He's right," she held up her hands to her friends' looks of surprise, "I'm certainly in no position to judge, I'm the worst person probably," she smiled at Shelby, "but there comes a time when it's our responsibility to live."

By the time they left the restaurant, all three of them were crying, but they shed happy tears.

Asher spent the next couple of days going over lesson plans for his class. Normally, he waited until the end of July or beginning of August to begin the task, but he was at his wits end; so frustrated from wanting Hannah, that he took on the detailed chore now.

History was his passion. He'd definitely gotten a lot of flack for having such a job, but the truth was, he didn't care. He loved it, learning about bygone eras and what the people did. Of course, he wasn't so blind that he didn't know that the current history books were full of inconsistencies and didn't always contain the things he himself thought that young minds should know. But, he did try to spice up the subject with interesting assignments and creative ways of testing the kids' knowledge.

Maybe he should take into account his own history? His history with Stella showed him what he didn't want. Now, there was Hannah, this beautiful, if not frustrating woman, and he was crazy about her.

History showed him that he'd never felt like this with any woman before now, and it was very complicated.

He was in the middle of planning his lesson plan when his phone went off. It was a text from Hannah,

Do you want to meet?

The question, although cryptic, was easily answered. He typed back,

YES!!!!!!!!

Hannah smiled at Asher's response. She'd spent the last couple of days researching local colleges, going over what she wanted to do, and thinking a lot about her parents.

Up until now, she'd basically separated them, her mother having passed away so long ago, and now her father. But they were together now, and that fact brought her more comfort than she thought it would. She didn't feel as alone as she feared she would. And, most of that was because of Asher and Skyler.

Before she could text him, Asher sent her a text saying,

When and where? Please make it soon!

His eagerness made her smile. She sent a reply,

Tonight, my place, 7pm, you have the address.

Asher read the text, dropped his lesson plans, and went upstairs to get ready.

Hannah ran around the house, cleaning things that didn't need cleaning and stressing out about what Asher would think of her house. It certainly wasn't as grand as his, but it was in a good neighborhood. She changed clothes about four times, not sure what she should wear.

Asher was about to leave the house when his phone rang. He looked at it and saw his parents' number. Since Skyler was with them, he answered with a quick, "Hello."

Brenda Kelley was upset, "Asher, it's your father, we're taking him to the hospital. Can you meet us?" She asked her son.

"What's wrong?" Asher got into his car as he was speaking to his mom. He pushed the garage door opener.

Crying, Brenda told him, "I think it might be a heart attack, we're going in the ambulance now and Skyler is scared."

As he pulled out of his driveway, Asher asked his mom, "Which hospital?"

Pacing her living room, Hannah was getting worried. It was seven-thirty and Asher still hadn't arrived. She didn't know if he was a person who was prompt but he didn't seem like someone who ran late. She'd tried to call him several times, but his phone went straight to voicemail. The doorbell rang, and Hannah sighed in relief.

She walked over, opened the door, and said, "It's about time, I missed you....." her words teetered off when she saw that it was Chris, her father's hospice caregiver, at the door and not Asher. "Chris," She said quickly, "I thought you were someone else."

Chris looked at her, hurt. "And here I thought you'd finally come around." He shoved flowers towards her, saying, "I got these for you."

If she wasn't so worried about Asher, Hannah would've seen how upset Chris was, but she didn't notice.

Stepping forward, so Hannah was forced to step backward, Chris all but forced his way inside. "Are you seeing someone?" He asked, an edge to his voice.

It was then that Hannah understood what was going on. He was most definitely confused about where they stood, and she started to feel a little trickle of fear go up her spine.

Taking Hannah's arm, Chris walked farther into the room, and closed the door behind them. He looked around, his face contorting into a grimace when he saw the living room. "You changed it!" He yelled.

Fear was settling into Hannah's chest. "I, uh, I wanted a new start," She returned, trying to sound calmer than she felt.

Leaning toward her, Chris clenched his jaw, and said, "You are supposed to do that with me."

Swallowing hard, Hannah tried to keep her mind from panicking. It took real effort. "Chris, you need to leave now."

He looked at her, as if he didn't see her. "Why?" He asked.

"Because you're scaring me," Hannah told him point blank. She wouldn't hold back.

Shaking his head, Chris asked her, "Scaring you?" He was offended at her words, "You won't talk to me, your dad told me what to do," he shot back, and tried to drag her toward the stairs.

Knowing now what he was planning, Hannah's self-preservation kicked into gear. "No!" She yelled, and leapt for the front door. She managed to get it open and screamed, "Help!!!!" as loud as she could.

Luckily, her neighbor, Richard, was outside watering his plants, and heard her. He came running over, saw the man who used to take care of Frank, trying to push Hannah inside. He slammed the door open and grabbed him. "What the hell do you think you're doing?" He yelled at the younger man while he shoved him outside onto the front walkway. "Hannah, call 911," He told her, and tackled Chris, who was now trying to run away.

Within minutes, the police were at her house. Chris was in handcuffs, and tucked into the back of a police car. Richard was with one officer, giving his statement, and she was with another, giving hers.

An hour later, the police had a tow truck there to tow Chris' car away, and he was taken to the police station for charges of attempted rape and assault.

Hannah watched the police leave and stood in the doorway of her house, numb.

Richard came over, with his wife, Heather, who asked Hannah, "Do you want to come over to our place?"

Shaking her head no, Hannah tried to smile. It was a small one, and didn't reach her eyes, but she appreciated their kindness. "No," She answered, and looked at Richard, "I want to say thank you." Trying to keep the tears at bay, Hannah said, "I don't know what would have happened."

They all knew what Chris would have done, given the chance.

"Well, I was there," Richard told her, "and it's funny because I was thinking of your dad when I went outside."

Hannah looked at him, and then asked, "Why?"

Richard shrugged, "I don't know really, I had this thought that he would be making fun of how bad the front yard looks, and thought I'd go water it."

Heather hugged Hannah, "We're right next door if you need us," she whispered.

She stood in the doorway, watching her neighbors go home, and Hannah thanked her father for looking out for her.

Asher was in the waiting room of the hospital when he looked at his phone. They'd been there for hours, waiting on the results of the tests the doctors ran. He saw that Hannah had called him a few times, and cursed himself for forgetting their date.

He looked up to see his mom come out with the doctor. He stood up, as did his sister and brother-in-law.

Brenda waited until they were near the kids, to say, "It was a mild heart attack," she said, and tried to remain calm. She knew her children would have questions so she asked the doctor to come out with her so he could answer them. She couldn't do it, not with Henry in the hospital bed, hooked up to machines.

Asher and his sister, Bethany, asked numerous questions. The doctor answered them efficiently. His demeanor led them to believe it was not as serious as they feared. When he left them, both Asher and his sister hugged their mom.

Skyler was sleeping on the waiting room sofa so, after making sure his mom was okay, Asher picked her up and took her home.

He got home about midnight, put Skyler to bed, and then remembered that he needed to contact Hannah. He sent a quick text, it wasn't appropriate, since he should call, but he didn't want to wake her.

I'm sorry I missed our date, family emergency.

After locking up the house, he checked his phone, and wasn't surprised when there was no response.

Hannah was crouched down, sobbing, in the corner of her closet. It was the only place she felt safe. About an hour after Richard and Heather left her at the house, she started to panic. She checked all the windows and doors, at least three times, and was still afraid that Chris would come back. Finally, she grabbed a blanket and went into her closet. Tucked into the corner, she felt some semblance of security. It was a long time before she fell asleep, her dreams contorted with fear and confusion.

With the closet door closed, it was still dark when Hannah woke up. She moved, and moaned. Whatever position she slept in wasn't too comfortable and her body was now resisting. It took a good ten minutes to get up and come out of the closet.

The sun shone brightly through the windows, and she squinted at the bright light.

Her bedside clock said eight a.m. Still feeling tired, Hannah used the bathroom, and went back to bed.

This time, she slept deeply, her dreams filled with her parents looking happy in Heaven. She begged them to take her with them, but they kept saying no. When she woke up later, she felt the tears she cried during her dreams.

It was hours later, when she came downstairs. She crept down the stairs, fearful of anything being out of place. Walking around the house, slowly, Hannah checked for anything out of the ordinary. When she was assured that everything was okay, she went into the kitchen to try and find something to eat.

Asher tried to call Hannah for the tenth time. He'd started about nine in the morning, not wanting to wake her up too early. After the fourth call, he started leaving messages. They were explanations really, telling her that his father had a heart attack, that he needed to be with his family, and that he needed to bring Skyler home late.

Now, he was just getting angry. At the very least, she could pick up the phone. His last message was a short, "Call me please."

Skyler came into the den, and asked him, "Daddy, is Grandpa going to be okay?"

His mind shifting to his daughter, Asher motioned her to come over to him. He set her on his lap, and told her, "Grandpa is going to be okay, as long as he does what Grandma and the doctor tell him."

Very seriously, Skyler responded, "I'm not sure he'll be okay then, Grandma says he NEVER listens to her."

Skyler's inflection of the words made Asher want to laugh for the first time today. He told her, "Well, we'll help him out then, okay?"

After she ran off, to play outside with the neighborhood kids, Asher called to check on his dad. His mom said he was sleeping peacefully and that the doctor would be sending him home the next day if he behaved. Asher relayed the conversation that Skyler and he had, and that made his mom laugh. They hung up a few minutes later.

Hannah was now back into his brain, making him wonder what she was doing…..

Standing in her kitchen, Hannah couldn't remember why she'd come into the room. "It's a kitchen," She reprimanded herself, "you came in here to eat." The problem was, she had absolutely no appetite at the moment.

The house was quiet, too quiet, so she went outside. Heather was in their yard, and noticed her. "Hannah," She smiled. But as she walked closer, her smile faded. "Oh my Lord," She whispered, and took Hannah by the shoulders and led her over to their house.

Chapter 21

Shelby was on her way to Hannah's house.

She hadn't heard from her friend in almost a week. After texting Payton, who said the same thing, she started to worry. It wasn't as if they'd known each other that long, but they texted pretty regularly since their trip to Galveston and something felt wrong to Shelby.

After pulling up in front of a nice looking, two-story house, Shelby looked around. Everything seemed nice and quiet.

She got out of her car and walked up to the door to ring the doorbell. No answer. She rang it again and knocked with her hand as well. A few seconds passed and then there was a sound from inside. The curtain on the window to the left of the door moved slightly. 'Good girl,' Shelby thought. Then the door opened and Shelby got a good look at Hannah. "Oh my God, what happened?" She demanded of Hannah.

Hannah knew she didn't look good, but the look on Shelby's face spoke volumes, none of it good. "I'm fine," She returned, quietly.

"You are most definitely not fine, Hannah, what's going on?" Shelby walked inside as Hannah stepped aside.

The house was tidy and neat, so that was something in Shelby's mind. She walked over to the sofa, sat down, and motioned for Hannah to join her. When Hannah was seated, Shelby asked again, "What happened?"

Even though days had passed since Chris' attack, Hannah couldn't seem to get herself on an even emotional path. "I'm not sleeping well," She answered, to which she received a 'don't give me that' look. "I," She started to say, and the tears just came pouring out.

Shelby held Hannah for a long time. It was a hunch, but Shelby had the distinct impression that this wasn't about grieving for her father's death. It felt way different, and Shelby should know, she'd been dealing with Kent's death for a while now. "Okay, spill," She crooned to Hannah.

The words didn't come easy at first, but eventually Hannah was able to open up. "And I was expecting Asher, when I opened the door, it was Chris." She explained, "He was the guy who took care of my dad while he was here in hospice. He was always so nice and I never got a weird feeling from him, before now."

Nodding, Shelby urged her to go on.

"Anyway, he just walked in, saw that I'd gotten new furniture in here, and basically went ballistic." She started crying again, the fear was as real now as it was then, "He started pushing me towards the stairs, and I knew what he was going to do," She could barely talk, she was crying so hard now.

Being forward, Shelby asked, "Hannah did he rape you?"

Shaking her head quickly, Hannah replied, "No, but he was planning on it, I'm sure of it. Luckily, I got to the door, and screamed. My neighbor, Richard, was outside, heard, and came running over. He was in the Army I guess, and took Chris down as if he were a rag doll." She smiled at that memory. "I was just so scared," She told Shelby.

Hugging her friend, Shelby returned, "I'll bet," she ran her fingers over Hannah's hair, "but why haven't you been returning our texts or calls?" she asked.

Confused, Hannah stared at her friend blankly, before saying, "I didn't get any."

"Honey," Shelby told her, "we've been texting and calling you for almost a week."

It dawned on Hannah, finally, that she hadn't even looked at her phone since the incident with Chris. She looked around the room absently, before murmuring, "I, uh, I don't know where my phone is."

Looking around the room herself, Shelby asked, "You don't know where your phone is, honey?"

Hannah nodded.

"Let's look for it then," Shelby told her.

The two of them stood up and started doing a more thorough search. Hannah went upstairs to search her room, while Shelby stayed downstairs and checked the kitchen, den, and living room. Pulling out her own phone, Shelby dialed the number to Hannah's phone and listened. She heard a buzzing sound and bent down to look under the oversized chair there, and located the missing phone. She shouted upstairs, "Hannah, I found it!"

Hannah came back down, and took the phone Shelby was holding up. She looked down and saw the caller ID said 25 missed calls and 42 texts. "Oh, geez," Hannah said in a breathless voice. She also saw the battery was low so she plugged it into an outlet in the kitchen. "I can't listen to all of them and return all those texts," She told Shelby, "it's too much."

"Okay, you go upstairs and shower," Shelby told her, "we'll go out to lunch. If it's okay with you, I'll go through them, take notes, and you can decide which ones you want to answer."

Feeling deflated, Hannah nodded, and said, "Thank you," to her friend, before going upstairs to shower.

Shelby watched her leave the room, then turned toward the counter and started to listen to voicemails.

She frowned when she heard the voicemails from Asher. At least now she understood why he didn't show up for his and Hannah's date. She also read his texts, and they seemed very apologetic. There were the numerous texts and calls from her and Payton, which she deleted. Hannah didn't need to feel guilty about not returning them. She sent Payton a text from her own phone explaining what happened. Payton texted her back immediately,

Oh, my Lord, tell her I'm thinking of her. If you need anything, call me!

Shelby continued to listen to voicemails and sighed when she heard the last one. It was just left this morning, and it was from a lady named Ms. Jasper.

Hannah was coming downstairs, and felt a lot better since she showered, did her hair, and put on some nicer clothes. While she was up in the bathroom, she realized that just having someone else in the house made her feel better. She didn't feel the fear that had been gripping her for the last six days. Smiling, for the first time, she walked into the kitchen, and told Shelby, "I feel a lot better, thank you for coming over."

Nodding, Shelby responded, "You look great!" Then she held up Hannah's phone, and told her, "There was a call from a Ms. Jasper about tomorrow night, your dad's dedication."

Closing her eyes, Hannah sighed. She'd forgotten about that. "Oh, yes," She smiled at Shelby, "I'm donating money to the high school for new baseball equipment, and they wanted to do something special for Dad."

Surprised that Hannah hadn't mentioned it before, Shelby asked, "Do you want Payton and I to come with you?"

Hannah nodded eagerly, and asked, "Would you? That would be great!"

Smiling, Shelby nodded in return. Then her smile fell and she explained, "There are a lot of voicemails and texts from Asher on your phone and I think you need to listen to them."

Reluctantly, Hannah walked to where the phone was sitting on the counter. "I will," She replied, "but after we eat lunch. I just want to get out of here."

Shelby grabbed her purse, smiled at Hannah, and said, "Okay, let's go."

They went to a local diner and had a nice lunch. Hannah didn't realize that keeping herself holed up in the house was actually making her feel worse. She was lucky that nothing happened with Chris, and that was what she should be focusing on. "I'm sorry, Shelby," She told her friend while they waited for their orders.

"For what?" Shelby asked back, "It's not like you didn't just go through something traumatic and couldn't pick up the phone to call your friends." Her sarcasm was blatant.

Smiling, Hannah replied, "I know, it's just that being so alone seems to be doing more to undermine the process of getting through my grief."

Shelby understood, perfectly. "I know, Hannah, we're all doing it here and there. We want to be done with it, but the truth is, it's damn hard."

Tears started falling down Hannah's cheeks, "He was so proud of me," she thought of her dad, and let the pain fill up her chest, "he wanted me to do what made me happy."

"Do you know what that is?" Shelby asked softly.

Smiling at her friend, Hannah answered, "You, Payton, Asher, and Skyler for starters," she squeezed Shelby's hand. "And going back to school to figure out what I want to do, that will help."

Not wanting to be the bad guy, but knowing someone had to ask the hard questions, she asked Hannah, "And about Asher and Skyler?"

Hannah sighed, "I know you said he left a lot of voicemails and texts so I'll read and listen first, and then decide what to do."

Their food came so they both ate. Hannah realized this was the first real meal she'd eaten in almost a week. No wonder she felt so warn down!

After their lunch, Shelby dropped Hannah off at the house, with the promise that she and Payton would be there to take her to the ceremony the next evening.

When Shelby pulled out of the driveway, Hannah went inside and sat down on the sofa. Her phone still needed charging but she wanted to hear what Asher left on it. She read the texts first,

Hannah, where are you? I was at the hospital with my family and left you messages. I understand if you're mad, but please call or text me back.

She felt awful, but had to read the rest. The next one read,

I get that you're mad, but please contact me.

Even though it was a text, she could see that he was becoming frustrated. The next texts were much the same, asking her to contact him, but getting shorter. She read down to the last one, and started crying,

It's apparent that my explanation of events wasn't good enough for you. My family has to be a priority. I thought you would understand that, after all you did for your father, but maybe you think that doesn't apply to me. I'm sorry to have bothered you.

That text pretty much said it all. He was done with her, and Lord knew, Hannah couldn't blame him. She had her own reasons and yet, they seemed so unimportant right now. But he was right, she should understand that his family was important, and she did.

Without listening to them, Hannah deleted all the voicemails. She didn't think it mattered anymore since Asher made it clear that their relationship was over.

She walked into the office, her chest heavy with emotion, and caught up on her emails. Ms. Jasper asked that she prepare something to say for the next evening, and that made Hannah anxious. What should she say? Getting up from the desk, she went over to the picture that was on the shelf, the one of her dad and her, and she studied it again. After a few minutes, the words started forming in her mind.

The next day, the nerves started in. Ms. Jasper didn't tell her how many people would be at the dedication, so she just

Danette Fogarty

assumed that it would be just the baseball coaches. But, she started getting calls from her father's friends, who told her they would be going. By the time she supposed to start getting ready, she was an emotional mess.

Payton and Shelby showed up a little early, and helped her with her hair and makeup. She decided to go with a black dress, not so much as a sign of mourning as it was the only dress that looked nice enough for her to wear.

With Payton doing her hair, Hannah winced at the tugging and pulling. "Hey, leave some in there, will you?" She asked jokingly.

Giving Hannah a silly look, Payton told her, "You have gorgeous hair, but there's a lot of it, and to get it all up and staying will take work, and a significant amount of pain on your part."

The dry tone Payton used made Shelby laugh. "Stop it, I'm trying to do makeup here and if I laugh, I may poke Hannah in the eye."

Their joking settled Hannah down significantly. There was nothing like friends to make you forget your worries. She'd forgotten that over the years, since taking care of her dad basically alienated her from all of her old friends. "Thank you both again," She said to them.

Giving Hannah's hair a tug, Payton replied, "You're welcome, now stop thanking us and let us help you look stunning."

Hannah dutifully sat there and let them continue their efforts. When she looked in the mirror, she was shocked by the transformation. Her hair was full, curly, and twisted into a complicated style that made her look like a model. The makeup Shelby did all but made Hannah's gaunt face glow. "Wow!" She sighed.

Looking pleased with themselves, Payton and Shelby gave one another a high five and stared at Hannah's reflection with satisfaction.

They left a few minutes earlier than Hannah planned so they could find where they were supposed to go.

Once they reached the parking lot, outside the high school gymnasium, they all wore a look of shock. The parking lot was packed! There had to be a hundred cars there.

Shelby drove, and pulled into the parking lot. They were met by a high school boy, who held up a sign saying, Hannah Whitman. Putting down her window, as she drove up beside him, Shelby told him, "We've got Ms. Whitman with us."

He nodded, and pointed to a spot close to the building, "We've reserved a parking spot for her, just pull up there."

With a nod, Shelby started driving again.

They parked two minutes later and all three sat in the car. Hannah was in the front passenger seat. Shelby and Payton were just waiting for her.

"I can't do this," Hannah said in a whisper. Her palms were sweaty and she was scared.

Leaning forward, Payton put her hand on Hannah's shoulder, and told her, "They are here to show their support, you just go in, give them the money, say a few words, and we're at the nearest bar within minutes."

Hannah laughed, "Okay," she answered, and opened the door.

They were walking inside when a woman approached them, and asked, "Are you Hannah Whitman?"

Hannah nodded, and smiled. "Ms. Jasper?" She asked in return.

Nodding yes, Ms. Jasper shook Hannah's hand, "We're so honored you could join us."

Following, the now moving, Ms. Jasper Hannah thought it was funny since SHE was the one who called Ms. Jasper in the first place about the donation. Looking behind her, she shrugged at Payton and Shelby.

They walked into the auditorium, and Hannah stopped. It was full of people. And when they saw her, they all stood up.

Hannah felt as if she were in some slo-mo sequence in a movie, she moved forward between the rows of chairs, and was greeted by her dad's friends and co-workers. Some she recognized, and some she didn't. It was overwhelming to see the number of people who came tonight and Hannah did her best to be polite and not to cry.

Ms. Jasper led her to the front row, where there were four chairs marked Reserved. She motioned for Hannah and her friends to take a seat and then walked over to where a raised podium was placed. She started to speak,

"Good evening, and welcome to our annual coaches meeting." There were a few chuckles from the crowd. "Usually we just get together at the local diner and go over our budget, schedule, training roster, etc., but I received a call a few weeks ago from Frank Whitman's daughter, Hannah. She asked me if she could donate money to the baseball program here at the high school. Since I'm a coach and a teacher, of course I said yes." A few more chuckles. "Frank Whitman was a coach here at the high school for more than twenty years. He was passionate about the game of baseball and, as he never was able to make it to the big leagues, decided to try and teach others." She smiled at Hannah, "When I told the other coaches about this, they started telling other teachers, and pretty soon, it was clear that Frank needed a little more than a few minutes at the local diner." Looking behind her, Ms. Jasper pointed to a large projector screen and said, "This is our tribute to Frank….."

Hannah sat there, stunned, as pictures of her father were shown on the large screen. The first ones were of his first years at the high school. She could hear people whispering, some recognized themselves or commented about her dad. It felt so good to know how much he was loved. The last year of his life, he refused to have any visitors, telling Hannah that he just didn't want people to see him so debilitated. Now she could understand why. He was so full of life, and these pictures showed it.

The pictures were almost to the end of her dad's career coaching, when she felt Payton tense, and heard her gasp. Looking over at her friend, Hannah asked, "Are you okay?"

Nodding quickly, Payton answered, "Uh, yeah, just recognized an old friend."

'Odd,' Hannah thought, the man who Payton called an old friend looked strangely familiar. She'd seen him before but couldn't recall where. Her mind was thrust back to the present when the lights came back up and Ms. Jasper said, "Now, Frank's daughter, Hannah would like to say a few words.

The applause was deafening, and Hannah took a deep breath before standing up. She made her way to the podium and gave Ms. Jasper a small smile. Luckily she'd written down what she had to say. Clearing her throat, she began,

"First of all, I'd like to thank everyone who could be here tonight. Dad wasn't one to make a show of things, except if he thought one of his players was being treated unfairly by the umpires." A few laughs came from the audience. "But, he loved baseball. He loved to teach, he loved to read, he loved to learn, and he loved to help others learn. At his funeral, I was approached by a good many of his former students who told me what he did to help all of them. It was humbling, because I really only knew him as Dad." She had to stop and take a deep breath to keep her emotions at bay. "But, he was a great many things to a great many people and he is probably up there," She pointed to the ceiling, "coaching a game right now. I would like to make this donation of $5000.00 to the high school baseball program to be used for new equipment. I would like to thank all of you who were students of my father's teachings, on or off the baseball field, because you made it so worthwhile for him. Thank you."

Hannah handed the check to Ms. Jasper, and expected to go back to her seat. But the whole auditorium stood up and was clapping so she just stood there, smiling. And, over the back of her shoulder, she thought she heard her dad say, "Good job."

Chapter 22

Asher was sitting at his parents' house, sulking. He promised his mom he'd come over and stay with his dad while she went out with his sister. They were invited to some function, he didn't know what, and he didn't know where it was so he just showed up at the appointed time. Skyler was staying over at a neighbor's house for a summer sleepover so he was glad to go over and keep his dad company. He hated being in the house alone, and especially hated being in his bedroom, because it reminded him of Hannah.

His dad was sitting in his recliner, in the living room, and just turned on the news. "Have a seat," He said to his son, "I'm sorry you have to babysit."

Smiling, Asher told his dad, "I don't mind," but his voice fell flat.

Looking at his son, Henry tried to comfort him by saying, "I know you still haven't talked to Hannah yet, because I think you'd look a lot happier if you had."

Nodding to his dad, Asher replied, "Maybe."

Henry rolled his eyes, "Really? You aren't going to try that 'I'm a big, strong guy who doesn't need a woman' crap on me are you?"

In the thirty years that Asher lived, he'd never had his dad say something like this to him. "Excuse me?" He asked, not really sure what else to say.

"Please," Henry said sarcastically, "You think I don't know that this Hannah girl turns you inside out. Hell, boy, why do you think I've been married to your mother so long? It's not because she's a good cook, because we both know that's not it," he leaned toward his son, "And if you tell her I said that, I'll deny it."

Now, Asher laughed. "So Mom turns you inside out?" He asked, then wished he hadn't because it sounded weird.

Henry huffed, "That woman has had me wrapped around her finger since day one," he held up one finger to demonstrate the point, "I couldn't think about anyone else and even when she infuriates me, which is pretty regularly, I love her even more."

"I just know I'm going to regret this next question, but I gotta ask dad," Asher sighed, "How did you know that you couldn't be without her?"

Turning, so he could face his son directly, Henry told him, "It wasn't that I couldn't be without her, son, it was that I didn't want to be without her, not for one damn day."

Asher thought about the words his dad used, not "couldn't" but "didn't want to." He knew in his own mind that he would live a perfectly nice life without Hannah, but it wouldn't be as wonderful as if she were in it. He was about to ask his dad something when he saw how intently his dad was looking at the television. Was that Hannah? He asked his dad, "Can you turn it up please?"

Henry turned up the volume and it was the sports edition of the news. The sportscaster was saying, "In local news, former Alvin High School baseball coach, Frank Whitman, was honored last night. His daughter, Hannah, thanked all of his students for inspiring her father. Coach Whitman is most notable for coaching Astros short stop, Sebastian Trent."

"I knew it!" Henry said enthusiastically, "Remember, I told you and your mom that Frank coached some big league hot shot."

Asher's eyes were still glued to the television because there was a video of Hannah. She looked gorgeous! His eyes were studying every bit of her.

Henry looked at his son, and then back to the television, and asked, "Is that her?"

Since he couldn't answer, Asher just nodded his head yes.

"Wow, she's beautiful," Henry commented.

Not thinking about his words, Asher replied, "She's more beautiful in person."

The tone his son used, Henry thought, was the same one he used when he and Brenda first got together. "Son," He waited until Asher looked at him, before saying, "I see a lot of things we can use as obstacles; our jobs, our circumstances, in your case you could even use Skyler, not on purpose, but you don't want to see your little girl hurt." He sighed, and added, "So I don't think, with what your mother has told me, what Skyler has said, and with what I see in your eyes right now, that you should let any obstacles get in the way of you being with that woman." He pointed at the television screen.

His dad's words were brilliant! Asher knew that, but he was still reluctant. He hadn't heard from Hannah in almost a week and, with the explanation of why he missed their date, he couldn't understand her freezing him out like that. "I'll try," He told his dad.

Henry frowned. His son certainly didn't look or sound like someone who would try. He'd make a note to talk to Brenda about this when she got home.

Asher got home and had a lot of time to think about what his dad said. When his mom got home, she asked him a dozen questions about his father, and Asher answered them exactly how his dad told him to. When his mom kissed him goodnight, she whispered, "Be happy," in his ear.

What would make him happiest was if Hannah would call or text him. If he knew that they could talk about this, hell if they could talk about anything, he'd be thrilled.

He went to bed that night with a heavy heart, and more questions than answers about his feelings for Hannah.

The day after her father's remembrance ceremony, Hannah's phone was ringing off the hook. Apparently it made the local news and was broadcast on all the local stations. She was glad the school and the baseball program got some exposure, but she was too worried about what classes to sign up for in the fall to notice how big the news of it actually was.

She'd sat down at the computer and looked over her college credits from eight years earlier. As long as they didn't expire, she didn't see why her previous credits wouldn't transfer. Since the situation with Chris, who was thankfully receiving some much needed care at a local psychiatric facility, she really thought about a comment Payton made to her at the house in Galveston.

During their dinner, Payton mentioned that Hannah would be a good counselor. At the time, Hannah assumed that her friend was probably joking, but now she found herself thinking about the possibility of that career path. She wanted to help families who had sick loved ones. There were positions in the local area and in hospice services for such people and Hannah loved the idea of helping people.

There were a few places in Houston that offered a degree in social work, and even some colleges that offered on-line degrees. She could do some volunteer work while she finished up her general studies, and then see how that went.

The plan wasn't solid, yet, but it was coming together. Hannah thought that was half the battle, getting back into the game.

Her phone pinged. It was a text from Shelby,

Just saw you on the news, you looked stunning. Really, Payton and I should do your hair and makeup more often.

Hannah laughed at the text, then replied,

Anytime.

She was about to go back to her online researching for her degree, when her phone pinged again. It was from Shelby again,

I said yes.

Getting excited, because that meant Shelby accepted a date with the uncle of one of her students, Hannah texted her back,

You did? When, where, what are you going to wear?

Hannah was sitting there, on pins and needles, until Shelby texted her back with,

Don't know, don't know, and for crying out loud, don't know

Shelby's sharp tongue, even in texts made Hannah laugh. Well, the least she could do was support Shelby in her effort to get back out there again, she typed back,

When you get the time and place, text Payton and me and we'll go shopping with you to find a new outfit.

There wasn't a response, so Hannah figured Shelby was off doing something else. She was happy for Shelby, finding a way to start getting on with her life, even if it was forced at first.

Hannah's mind drifted away from her task of finding classes, and settled on Asher. She wondered what he was doing. She wondered what he and Skyler were doing. She wondered if they were thinking about her as much as she was thinking about them. She reached for the phone, intent on calling him, but put it down at the last moment. It would do them no good to go on if she wasn't very sure about what she wanted.

Hannah slept well that night, for what she was dealing with anyway. Sleep was a subjective thing these days, so she was grateful for whatever rest her emotions allowed her body to get. Looking in the mirror, she knew she looked tired, with the bruises under her eyes. Feeling much older than her twenty-seven years, she went downstairs to try and get some coffee in her system and some energy to face the day.

She was at her computer, an hour later, when her phone rang. She didn't recognize the number, but the caller ID said it was Galveston, Texas so she answered with a tentative, "Hello."

"Hannah," Willa Hanson replied, "Thank goodness you're here, I just got a call from someone saying that Payton was coming here and she's very upset."

Her mind immediately on alert, Hannah asked, "What happened?"

Willa wasn't sure how much she could reveal, for that matter, how much she should reveal, but she knew that Hannah and Shelby were the closest friends Payton had these days. "From what I understand, there was some confusion and her daughter's room was cleared out."

Not understanding where any "confusion" could come into play, Hannah frowned. "What?" She asked, "Who would do that?"

Now Willa knew she couldn't say anymore. "I don't know any more than that, I only know she's coming here. I've called Shelby and she's on her way, can you come?"

"Of course," Hannah told Ms. Hanson, "I'll get there as soon as I can."

Asher's phone rang mid-morning. He didn't know who the caller was, but he answered. Maybe it was a new teacher who was reaching out for help? Sometimes the school gave out numbers for training purposes. "Hello," He said lightly.

"Asher?" A woman's voice asked.

This didn't sound like someone he knew. "Yes, it is, who is this?"

Shelby smiled, "This is Shelby Forrester," she cleared her throat, "I'm Hannah's friend from the Galveston Retreat."

Now he remembered, "Yes, Shelby," he responded, and asked, "How can I help you?"

The formality in his tone spoke volumes to Shelby. She figured Hannah would be too chicken to call him and explain what was going on. "Well, this call is to see if I can help you."

Confused, Asher asked, "Oh?"

The best way to say it, was to just say it plain; that was Shelby's policy. "The night of your date, when you didn't show up because your dad had a heart attack?" She asked, "How is he by the way?"

"He's fine," Asher answered, and inquired, "How did you know he had a heart attack?"

Too many questions, Shelby thought. "I listened to all of your voicemails and read your texts to Hannah."

This, he didn't care for. "Can I ask why you're calling me instead of Hannah?" He couldn't help that his anger was creeping into his words.

Sighing, Shelby explained, "I'm going to tell you everything, but I need you to just listen, okay?"

Asher nodded, then realized she couldn't hear that, so he said, "Yes, go on."

"Okay," Shelby started, "that night, that guy Chris, the one who was taking care of Hannah's dad for hospice…"

Interrupting her, Asher asked, "Isn't he the one who was harassing her?"

Relieved that Hannah had told him that much, Shelby replied, "Yes, well he decided to pay a visit. She thought he was you, just running late, and well, he tried to force himself on her."

Her words may have been PC, but Asher knew what she meant, "That son of a….." he started to say.

"Don't!" Shelby cut him off, "Nothing happened, thank God, Hannah was able to call for help and her neighbor came over and gave that jerk a good beat down and held him until the police arrived."

There was no way to describe the tumultuous feelings running through Asher at the moment. Hannah had been in trouble, and he wasn't there.

Shelby didn't hear him respond, so she went on to say, "She's okay, but her phone was dropped and slid under a living room chair during the incident," she tried to use more delicate words, "so she didn't answer anyone's calls or texts."

Dawning was making its way through Asher's thick skull, and he felt like the biggest ass in the world. "I see," He answered, because he didn't know Shelby well enough to give voice to all he felt at the moment.

His answer worried Shelby a bit, she wasn't sure if he was as serious about Hannah as she suspected. "Well, she's now back out at Galveston Retreat."

"Oh," Asher said in response.

Frustrated, Shelby sighed, and asked, "Do you love her?" Her voice was raised because she couldn't help defending her friend.

His anger was directed at this Shelby woman now, "Yes!" He shouted, "But she doesn't want to call me!"

There it was! That was the passion Shelby was hoping to find in Asher. "After what I just told you, do you think she feels like calling you up and chatting?" She shook her head at the ridiculousness of men, "She's trying to heal, you come along, sweep her up into this crazy love, and now, when she's alone and needs you, you just complain that she's not calling you?"

"How dare you!" Asher accused her. "I called, I texted, I want her here with me, with Skyler, in our lives! I told her not to leave here when she came up and stayed over. Hell, my dad told me not to let her go!" He couldn't help but rant, the feelings had been building up inside him since that day she left his house.

His outburst gave Shelby hope. She softened her voice, "Then why are we discussing this instead of you getting in your car and coming here to see her, comfort her, and love her?"

"Fine!" He answered, and shot out, "I'll be there as soon as I can!"

With a light, "See you then," Shelby hung up the phone. When she turned around, she saw a hopeful looking Ms. Hanson and Payton.

Payton asked, "Well?"

Shelby gave them a thumbs up, "He's on his way."

Willa shot the two of them a motherly look, and said, "I hope this works, if they get here and are mad that we've duped them into coming, it may backfire."

Sitting down at the kitchen table, Shelby shook her head no, "I know what I saw in her, Ms. Hanson. She loves him."

Joining Shelby, Payton nodded, "I got the same thing, every time she mentioned him or Skyler."

Deciding to agree with them, Willa asked, "And what about you two?" She smiled, "Here, you've gone and made it so your friend finds someone to help her heal, love, and move on, but what about you?"

Payton looked at Shelby, and smiled, before saying, "We're working on it Ms. Hanson."

Nodding in agreement, Shelby told the older woman, "Yes, we're working on it."

Hannah ran upstairs and jumped in the shower. She didn't even bother with her hair, instead she twisted it and secured it with a clip. 'How could anyone do that to Payton?' She asked herself for about the dozenth time. She didn't understand how someone could possibly misunderstand Payton's needs during this time. She was mourning for crying out loud!

Within ten minutes, she was in her car, headed for Galveston Retreat. She hadn't even texted Shelby because Ms. Hanson said she was on her way as well. Hannah just hoped that one of them could calm poor Payton down.

Asher hung up with Hannah's friend, and called his neighbor to ask if Skyler could stay over for another night. He didn't know how long this would take with Hannah and didn't want to worry about when he had to be back to get his daughter. His neighbor, Mary, told him that the kids were fine and to do whatever he needed to do.

Getting into his car, Asher pushed the Bluetooth button to call his parents' house. His mother answered, "Hello, Asher," and he didn't even greet her before asking, "Mom, can I talk to Dad?"

Brenda, surprised, quietly handed the phone to her husband. Henry greeted his son with, "Hey son, what's up?"

"Dad, you were right," Asher explained, "She ran into some drama of her own on the night I missed our date and now I'm going to Galveston to make sure she's okay."

Smiling, Henry instructed his son, "Now, don't be afraid to beg, they like that and it gets you sympathy."

Trying not to laugh, Asher answered, "Okay, I'll think about it," and disconnected the call.

Brenda gave her husband a questioning glare, and asked him, "What was that about?"

Feeling smug, Henry leaned over and kissed his wife, "That's our son going to get Hannah."

Putting her hands on her hips, Brenda asked, "What's this all about?"

Henry smiled, and explained the other evening when Asher was at their house. He was honest and told his wife exactly what he told their son.

With tears in her eyes, Brenda told her husband, "I don't want to be without you either, my love."

Chapter 23

Hannah drove too fast, and ended up spitting up gravel, as she pulled into the drive that led to the B&B. She was relieved to see Shelby's car parked there already.

After throwing the car into park, she almost ran up to the front porch, and was met by a worried looking Ms. Hanson.

"Where's Payton? How is she?" Hannah asked.

Ms. Hanson pulled her into a hug, and whispered, "Better, why don't you come inside?"

Maybe she misunderstood the situation? Ms. Hanson didn't sound as upset as she did when she called earlier. Maybe things had calmed down.

After following Ms. Hanson into the living room, and still not seeing either Shelby or Payton, Hannah began to worry. "Where is everyone?" She asked Ms. Hanson.

"Upstairs, in the room you used while you stayed here," Willa answered, and pointed upstairs.

For some reason, Hannah sensed that the usually no-nonsense Ms. Hanson was reserved. There was a funny feeling making its way through her gut, and she didn't care for it.

Going upstairs, Hannah slowed her pace. If there was one thing she knew, it was that if the situation was already under control, you didn't go into it with drama.

The door to the room she used still had the door hanger on that read Hannah, and she smiled. Ms. Hanson probably forgot to take it down after she left.

She knocked softly, then opened the door. Expecting to see Payton crumpled up on the floor, and Shelby comforting her,

Hannah was surprised when she didn't see anyone. Going through the room, she went out onto the patio. The door was open, the breeze from the Gulf was blowing the curtains, making them dance inside the room.

As she walked out onto the balcony, Hannah saw Shelby and Payton standing to one side. She frowned, because neither of them looked to be that upset. "What's going on?" She asked. "Ms. Hanson called me to say that Payton was here and very hurt and going crazy."

Sighing, Payton answered, "I am very hurt and upset, let's face it, we all are."

Taking her turn, Shelby piped up, "And we're all just trying to make our way through the feelings we have about losing our loved ones. You knew, Hannah, you knew he was going to die long before it happened." Tears started streaming down her face, as she said the words to her friend. "Neither of us knew, but you did."

Hannah's chest tightened with emotion. She knew what Shelby meant. "He told me," She choked out, "when I came home from college, he told me he was going to die from that stupid disease."

Payton added, "And you stayed, you stayed to take care of him because you loved him so much."

Nodding, Hannah whispered, and plopped down into a nearby chair, "Yes, he was my dad, my hero."

They were all crying now, and they knew it was necessary for them to move forward.

"I called Asher," Shelby admitted. "I told him about what happened with Chris."

Emotions danced across Hannah's face, she didn't know whether to be mad or glad because she didn't think she could ever tell him. "Why?" She asked.

Shelby stepped forward, and took Hannah's hand, "Because, my friend, you weren't going to." When Hannah started to shake her head in denial, but Shelby interrupted her, "We all know you wouldn't. You were ashamed and you were hurt that he didn't show up, even though we all know his reason was valid."

Hannah hated it when her own shortcomings were exposed. "You're right," She said defiantly, "but he could've called me too."

Now Payton stepped forward, "How was he to know?" She asked Hannah. "People can't read your mind, you know, he is just as confused as you are."

Denying it, Hannah retorted, "He doesn't understand."

"How can you say that?" Shelby asked, "His wife CHOSE to leave him, and that adorable little girl. She didn't even look back, from what you told me. None of us," She choked up, trying to get the words out, "none of us chose to have our loved ones leave us. At least we can understand that they didn't want to leave us, it was not their choice."

Now that Shelby explained it, Hannah felt so awful! She knew what her friends were saying, but it was still difficult to just pick up the phone and call him. "What do you want me to do?" She asked, and plopped down in the chair behind her.

Now Shelby smiled, "We want you to go down there," she pointed down to the beach, "and tell him everything that's in your heart."

Looking to her right, Hannah saw a person sitting down on the beach, alone. Her eyes widened and she looked back at her friends, "Is that him?"

Payton nodded, "Yes, and remember, he knows everything."

Hannah looked at Payton harshly, "You didn't need to tell him, you know!"

Looking back at Shelby, just as harshly, Payton hissed, "No secrets!"

Ms. Hanson stood in the doorway, tears streaming down her cheeks as she listened to what the three women were saying. It was beautiful, what was happening, and yet it broke her heart to see it. "Now," She interrupted them, and smiled when all three of them looked at her, "It's your turn to make a choice," she pointed out to the beach, "You can decide to go out there and talk to him and resolve this, or you can decide you don't want to." She looked at Payton and Shelby, "None of us will judge your decision." She smiled, "But we also won't accept it if you decide against taking this chance and then complain about it for the rest of your days."

Shelby looked at Payton, who was trying not to smile.

Hannah listened to them, torn between being mad and being so happy that she found them as friends. "I want to.....but,"

Willa put up her hands, "No excuses," her words were curt, "This is your life, you either take it or you leave it." She softened them now, "Just remember that love is the biggest gift you'll ever give and get, and it's worth it."

Nodding in agreement, both Payton and Shelby stepped forward, each offering a hand to Hannah.

Her decision made, Hannah allowed them to pull her up, and into a hug. Even Ms. Hanson joined in.

Ms. Hanson, Shelby, and Payton stayed there on the balcony as Hannah left the room to go down to the beach, and meet Asher where he sat on the beach.

They all stood there, leaning against the railing. It was tough to watch Hannah walk out there. They could see her reluctance, and fear.

"She's not going to chicken out, is she?" Shelby asked to no one in particular.

Chuckling, Payton nudged her friend with her shoulder, "Stop it! She'll be fine......I hope."

Smiling at the other two women, Willa offered, "If you have faith, it will all turn out okay."

Hannah thought the walk down to the beach was the longest walk she'd ever taken. It seemed to take hours for her to cross the backyard and go down the slope to reach the sand. She watched Asher the whole time, not being able to take her eyes off of him. He was sitting there, his shoulders slumped. She worried that it was because he'd given up on her.

Asher sat on the beach. He migrated between being pissed about the misrepresentation Shelby gave him about Hannah, and thankful that Hannah's friends wanted to intervene. She wasn't here when he arrived. He'd almost broken the front door, he pounded so hard on it. Shelby answered, invited him in, and asked him to sit down on the patio before she explained the truth of the situation.

He got up to leave, but Ms. Hanson asked him to stay. She told him about losing her husband and son, and he couldn't just leave after that. Instead, he went out to the beach, and told them that he would wait for Hannah.

So, here he sat, and wondered if she'd ever show up.

"Asher," Hannah said, when she was a few feet from him. Her heart skipped a beat when he turned to look at her. She could see him start to move, and put her hand up, "Stay sitting please," she said, crossed the few feet between them, and sat down beside him.

As soon as he heard his name, Asher's heartbeat sped up. She'd come to him! He smiled when he saw her, but stayed put when she asked him to.

They sat there for a few minutes, neither saying anything.

Finally, Hannah knew it would need to be her who instigated the conversation, so she started, "I'm sorry I didn't call you."

Asher simply nodded, but didn't say anything.

"After the thing with Chris," Hannah's voice faltered a bit, but she recovered, "I felt broken down. I didn't want to burden you with all of that and my inability to figure out what I want to do."

Again, he nodded, but didn't respond.

Sighing, Hannah clutched her hands together, she needed to gather her strength. "I left your house that day, after our night together, and felt so wonderful and sad at the same time."

Deciding to speak, Asher told her, "Because you didn't think you deserved to be happy when your dad just died."

It shouldn't have surprised Hannah that he understood, but it did anyway. "Yes."

"Do you think your dad would want you to mourn forever?" Asher asked her.

She shook her head no, answering, "No, he would be the first to say, even if you strike out a hundred times, you still take your next at bat."

Asher realized he would've really liked Hannah's dad, Frank, and learned a bit about him from his own dad. "And so, you're standing at the plate now," He kept up the metaphor, "Are you going to swing for the stands, or are you going to let the pitch just pass you by?"

Smiling, Hannah replied, "I would embarrass him and myself if I let such a sweet pitch pass me by."

Physically turning, Asher faced Hannah now. He reached his hand out, and was relieved when she placed hers into it. His palm covered hers, just like he wished his love could cover her whole being and protect her always. "We've both been banged up pretty good by life, Hannah. But I know that you are the best thing to happen to me, and I know Skyler adores you."

She let the tears fall down her cheeks. "I miss you both so much," she smiled through her tears, "I just felt so worn down and couldn't make any decisions. I didn't trust myself either because Chris seemed so nice and safe before, and now….." she let the words trail off.

Just the mention of that jackass's name made Asher more angry than he could remember being before. "And that," He started.

Hannah shut him down, "I know, I should've called you. I will tell you that he's getting help and that's what's important."

"But, what if?" Asher asked, emotion filling his voice.

Now it was Hannah's turn to be strong, "The what if's don't matter if it all turns out okay."

He could see her changing the subject, and loved her more for it. "Is it okay, Hannah?" He asked her.

She moved so they were sitting, face to face, "If I'm going to be with you, and Skyler, then it's all perfectly okay."

Adjusting, so he could pull out a piece of paper, he handed it to her.

Giving him a questioning look, Hannah accepted the paper and unfolded it. There was a picture, drawn in crayon, of a little girl and two adults. In a six year old's handwriting, there were arrows that said, Me, Daddy, My new mommy, Hana. She read the words and smiled.

"I guess we'll have to teach her how to write my name," Hannah told Asher.

He smiled, and asked, "Oh, you mean with the other n and h?"

Shaking her head no, Hannah answered, "No, with a capital M for Mommy."

Asher's breath caught. "Does this mean that you'll marry me, Hannah? Because I'm in love with you and I never want to be without you again."

Not answering his question, Ḥannah's heart was beating so hard she could hear it in her ears. Instead, she told him, "I'm going back to school to be a social worker."

She didn't answer his question so Asher started to get edgy. "That's good," He replied.

"Do you think I can manage being a full-time student, a wife, and a mother?" Hannah asked him, a sly smile on her face.

Rubbing his hands up and down her arms, Asher answered, "I think you can do absolutely anything you set your mind to."

Pretending to think hard, Hannah looked away for a few seconds, then, not wanting to make him wait too long, she responded, "Then I choose to be a full-time student, a wife to you, a mother to Skyler, and a friend to the three of those goofy looking women up there," and she pointed to the balcony where Ms. Hanson, Shelby, and Payton stood, watching them.

Asher wanted to jump for joy. "Do you love me?" He asked her, curious because she hadn't said the words yet.

Looking at him, this man who managed to heal her heart and make her feel more than she ever thought she could, Hannah smiled, and said, "I love you. I think I have from the very first moment when I saw you helping Skyler with that baby turtle."

Throwing his head back, and laughing, Asher told her, "I think it was that fast for me too, although I'll only admit that to you." He grew serious, "And I think your dad knew that I would be there to help you. You could say, he arranged it."

Hannah's expression grew serious in response to his words, she nodded, informed him, "I guess there's only two questions left then…."

Looking at her, trying to figure out what she meant, Asher asked, "What are those?"

"Number one, when are you going to kiss me?" Hannah whispered, and moved toward him.

Smiling himself, Asher gladly obliged her, leaning in and closing his lips over hers. She tasted like tears, and love, and happiness, and he knew in his heart that she would always be there.

The kiss was long, and slow, and full of love.

Asher pulled away first, realizing that she didn't tell him about the second question. He asked, "And number two?"

Hannah's smile was slow, taking its time to cover her face, transforming it into an almost devilish grin. "Where's the ring?"

For the second time, Asher laughed hard. Oh, she'd never let him get complacent. "That," He tapped her lips with his finger, and sighed with want when she nipped his finger with her teeth, "we'll have to do together."

"There isn't anything I want to do, from here on out, without you," Hannah told him, her voice filled with emotion.

His smile gone, replaced with his own emotion, Asher cupped her face between his hands, and told her, "You'll never have to."

The three women standing on the balcony were all crying the happiest of tears.

Payton spoke first, "Well, I guess she didn't screw up," receiving a reciprocating nudge from Shelby, and laughing.

Willa looked at the two of them, and wondered if they knew their own stories would be continuing. She silently left them on the balcony, and went downstairs to her computer.

To: Baseballguy2005@email.com, Ruthrobers@email.com

Subject: Hannah's Story

Well, you were right. I just watched Hannah and Asher make up and it looks like it will be wonderful for the two of them. I can report that Shelby has accepted a date with an uncle of one of her students. That sounds promising. And Payton, well, she is still in a lot of pain, but she's healing. This is a wonderful day and I'm glad that we decided to do this. Please take care.

Love,

Willa

Keep reading for an

excerpt of

Danette Fogarty's

new book

Shelby's Story;

Book 2:

Love After Loss Series

Shelby scrubbed the bathtub, and fumed with anger. Kent was late, yet again, and she was getting really tired of it. She understood that his job was his passion. She'd tried to be supportive hadn't she? She'd quit her job to help him run the gym, she'd been there for uniform fittings, doing the girls' hair, and helping calm more than one emotional gymnast after he'd given her a verbal blasting. She thought the least that he could do was be home, on time, for date night.

Now, she was cleaning their already clean bathroom, and he was going to pull into the driveway, get out, and give her the smile that always melted away the anger she was currently holding in her.

Smiling at the prospect of what she had planned for the evening, Shelby decided to forgive him in advance. She knew that the gym, thankfully, was really taking off. He had a few new athletes that held a lot of potential. They didn't dare say Olympics, but Shelby knew all the coaches were thinking it.

Gymnastics was an all-encompassing business. You loved it or hated it and Kent, well, he loved it with every fiber of his being. He loved the hours of hard work, loved trying to mold his gymnasts into the kind of competitors others would respect, and even fear a little.

The tub was now sparkling clean.

Shelby smiled because it was going to be filled with a bubble bath for two later on this evening.

Looking at her phone, she sighed. She tried to call him but it went straight to voicemail. She'd better get showered and changed. If he wasn't answering his phone, that meant he was on his way and she had approximately a half hour.

Using the shower, Shelby quickly got cleaned up. She pulled on a light sundress, put on some lip gloss and mascara only since Kent didn't like her to be too "done up." Her hair was already pulled back into a clip that would be easy to let loose later. She just finished putting on her perfume when the doorbell rang.

Strange, she thought. They weren't expecting anyone tonight.

Walking down the hallway toward the front door, Shelby thought she saw more than one person through the curtained window on the door. She wondered if Kent invited parents over to dinner. He did that on occasion when they were trying to get new gymnasts to come to the gym, but he always told her first.

As she opened the door, Shelby frowned. There were two police officers standing there on her front porch. "Hello?" She asked, sure they were at the wrong address.

The first officer, a woman, asked her, "Are you Shelby Forrester?"

Shelby nodded, and wondered why her skin was becoming prickly, the hairs on it standing up.

"Is your husband Kent Forrester?" The other officer asked, his voice a little squeaky.

Swallowing hard, Shelby answered him, "Yes, he is, what's going on?"

The woman officer stepped forward, "Mrs. Forrester, I'm Officer Simon, and this is Officer Franklin, may we come in for a moment?"

Still not knowing what this was about, Shelby silently nodded, and led them inside.

Officer Simon asked, "Why don't we sit down?"

Shelby was becoming more upset by the second. "Okay, you're scaring me," Her voice was becoming louder, "just tell me what's going on."

Looking at one another, the officers waited a couple of seconds, then Officer Franklin told her, "There was an accident on the freeway. A semi-truck was heading down the freeway and didn't see a dog that ran out. He tried to swerve to avoid the dog, and his vehicle went into the next lane, which he thought was empty. Your husband was on his motorcycle, so the driver of the semi-truck didn't see him. The truck struck his motorcycle and he was forced into another lane, and hit another vehicle."

As she was listening, Shelby's heart was beating in triple-time. Swallowing hard, she asked them, "What hospital is he at?"

The officers exchanged another look between them before Officer Simon stepped forward. She took Shelby's hand, and told her, "I'm sorry to tell you this, Mrs. Forrester, but the impact of your husband's motorcycle into the second vehicle was severe. I'm sorry to say that he expired at the scene."

'Okay, I'm having a nightmare,' Shelby told herself. 'Wake up, Shelby' she demanded of herself. 'Wake up!'

Officer Simon watched Mrs. Forrester, and knew the news wasn't taking root yet. She was in shock. "Let's sit down," She told the shaking woman, and joined her on the sofa. Looking at her partner, she instructed him, "Please get Mrs. Forrester some water," and watched as he left the room quickly.

No one wanted this kind of assignment.

Looking at the police woman next to her, Shelby asked, "Are you telling me that Kent is dead?"

Taking a deep breath, Officer Simon answered, "Yes, Mrs. Forrester, I am."